Mastering Campaign Trading for Volatile Markets:

Strategies for Selection, Adjustment & Success

With AI Support Examples

Tom Batchelor

Firebird Trading Systems, LLC

DISCLAIMER

This book is intended for informational and educational purposes only. The information presented in this book is not a substitute for professional financial or legal advice. The author and publisher make no representations or warranties of any kind, express or implied, about the completeness, accuracy, reliability, suitability, or availability with respect to the book or the information, products, services, or related graphics contained in the book for any purposes. Any reliance you place on such information is therefore strictly at your own risk.

The author may include affiliate links in this book. If you purchase a product or service through one of these links, the author may receive a commission. The presence of affiliate links does not affect the content, or recommendations made in this book. The author only includes affiliates for products or services that they believe will add value to the reader.

Please consult with a professional financial advisor or attorney before making any financial decisions. The author and publisher do not assume any responsibility for errors, inaccuracies, or omissions. They shall not be liable for any loss or damage of any kind, including but not limited to any direct, indirect, incidental, consequential, special or exemplary damages, arising from or in connection with the use of the book or the information contained within it.

Firebird Trading Systems

TABLE OF CONTENTS

Chapter: 1 1

Understanding Volatile Markets

Chapter: 2 16

Option Greeks in a Volatile World

Chapter: 3 35

Strategy Selection in Volatile Markets

Chapter: 4 49

Trading Pivots: Direction and Decay

Chapter: 5 59

Pivot Strategy Case Studies: Initial Set Up and Adjustments

Chapter: 6 74

Gamma Scalping Fundamentals – Strategy, Setup, and Selection

Chapter: 7 97

Executing and Managing the Dynamic Gamma Scalping Position

Chapter: 8 104

Gamma Scalping in Practice: A Real-World Example

Chapter: 9 113

Technical Analysis in Volatile Markets

Chapter: 10 119

Deep-In-The-Money Calls and Puts – Precision Tools for Volatile Campaigns

Chapter: 11 139

Final Thoughts on Trading in Volatile Markets

Appendices: 153

Appendix A 153

Firebird Trading Systems Products

Appendix B 154

Glossary of Option Trading Terms

Appendix C 157

Example Python Script to Find DITM Calls

PLEASE READ

TradeStation is making a special offer to those who buy this book.

Follow this QR Code to the TradeStation Offer page.

Scan me!

We hope that you enjoy trading at TradeStation!

Chapter: 1

Understanding Volatile Markets

Volatility is the heartbeat of financial markets—its rhythm shifting with the pulse of global events, investor sentiment, and structural market behavior. For campaign traders, understanding volatility is not just about bracing for storms—it's about harnessing that energy to craft smarter entries, more adaptive adjustments, and ultimately, better results.

The Truth is that competent campaign traders love market volatility.

A. What Defines Volatility in Markets and How It Manifests

Volatility represents the **magnitude and frequency of price fluctuations** in a financial asset over a specific time frame. In the context of options trading, volatility is **not only a measure of risk—but also a pricing engine,** directly impacting option premiums and strategic trade decisions.

Broadly, volatility captures the **uncertainty or variability** in an asset's returns. It reflects how much a security's price deviates from its average over time—and in volatile conditions, that deviation becomes more extreme, more sudden, and often more difficult to manage.

1. Types of Volatility: Historical vs. Implied

Historical (Realized) Volatility

- Based on actual past price movement.
- Typically measured by **standard deviation** or **variance** of returns over a selected period (e.g., 10-day, 30-day HV).
- Used to assess how turbulent a stock has been.

Metrics:

- Daily standard deviation
- **Annualized** HV (e.g., a 30% HV implies 30% expected annual movement)

Implied Volatility (IV)

- Forward-looking, derived from current option prices.
- Reflects **market expectations** for future volatility.
- Often higher during earnings season, economic reports, or geopolitical events.
- Traders compare **IV vs. HV** to evaluate whether options are **cheap or expensive.**

Metrics:

- **IV Rank** – Where the current IV stands relative to the past 12 months.
- **IV Percentile** – What percentage of time the IV was lower over a set period.

2. Additional Metrics and Models Used to Gauge Volatility

- **Beta:** Measures a stock's volatility relative to a benchmark index like the S&P 500. A beta >1 indicates higher-than-market volatility.
- **Average True Range (ATR):** A technical indicator that reflects the daily price range, including gaps. Useful for setting stop-losses and determining trade size.
- **Bollinger Band Width:** Measures expansion and contraction in price volatility using standard deviations.
- **Volatility Skew:** Shows how implied volatility varies across strike prices—used to detect directional sentiment and tail-risk pricing.
- **Volatility Surface:** A 3D view of IV across multiple strikes and expirations.
- **Expected Move (EM):** Derived from ATM straddle pricing, estimating how much the stock is expected to move by a certain date.

3. How Volatility Manifests in Price Action

Volatility reveals itself not just in numbers but in recognizable **market behaviors:**

- **Price Gaps:** Overnight or intraday moves caused by news, earnings, or sentiment shifts.
- **Sharp Intraday Reversals:** "Whipsaw" conditions where price rapidly shifts direction.
- **High-Volume Trend Days:** Markets surge or collapse without retracement, driven by momentum and emotion.
- **Range Expansion:** Breakouts from consolidation zones with increased volume and volatility.
- **Compression Breakouts:** Periods of tight-range congestion that explode when volatility reenters.

In options trading, these manifestations affect **delta, gamma**, and **theta behavior**, especially near strike prices and expiration dates.

B. Why It Matters to Traders

Understanding volatility helps traders to:

- **Time entries and exits** with greater precision
- **Adjust position sizing** based on expected range and risk
- **Select the right strategy**: high IV for Decay-based, low IV for Directional-based spreads
- **Manage risk proactively**, especially in campaign trading or multi-leg diagonal strategies

For campaign-style traders, volatility is both the terrain and the tool. Recognizing how and when it changes provides a key advantage in structuring, adjusting, and exiting trades profitably.

C. Common Causes of Market Volatility: Economic, Political, Structural, and Geopolitical

Market volatility does not occur in a vacuum. It often arises from external catalysts that inject uncertainty, disrupt trends, and force traders to reassess risk and pricing. These catalysts can be grouped into four broad categories, each capable of triggering sharp movements, increased implied volatility, and wider bid-ask spreads across asset classes.

1. Economic Catalysts

Economic volatility stems from the release of macroeconomic data and central bank decisions that affect the outlook for growth, inflation, and interest rates. These catalysts influence not just broad indices, but also sector-specific and company-specific valuations.

Key Examples:

- **Interest Rate Decisions (Federal Reserve, ECB, etc.):**

A surprise rate hike or dovish pause can rapidly shift bond yields, equity valuations, and currency strength.

Example: *The Fed's rapid rate hikes in 2022 triggered a multi-sector selloff and elevated VIX readings.*

- **Inflation Reports (CPI, PPI):**

Higher-than-expected inflation often leads to expectations of tighter monetary policy.

Example: *A hot CPI print can send the market into a tailspin within minutes of release.*

- **Jobs Data (Non-Farm Payrolls, Unemployment Claims):**

Labor market strength or weakness affects rate policy and spending confidence.

Example: *A much stronger-than-expected payroll number may increase fears of persistent inflation.*

- **GDP Releases:**

Indicates whether an economy is growing or contracting—key to equity and commodity pricing.

Example: *A negative GDP print could confirm recession fears, spiking downside hedging activity in options.*

2. Political Catalysts

Political developments introduce policy uncertainty and can significantly shift investor sentiment, particularly in regulated or government-sensitive sectors such as healthcare, energy, and defense.

Key Examples:

- **National Elections:**

Changes in leadership or control of legislative bodies can impact fiscal spending, taxation, and regulation.

Example: *The 2016 U.S. presidential election caused extreme overnight volatility in futures and sectors like defense and tech.*

- **Regulatory Shifts:**

Proposed or enacted laws that target industries or financial practices.

Example: *Sudden antitrust investigations into tech giants can send those stocks sharply lower.*

- **Leadership Transitions or Scandals:**

Political instability—especially in emerging markets—can lead to foreign capital flight.

Example: UK Prime Minister changes in 2022-23 triggered bond and currency volatility.

3. Structural Catalysts

Structural volatility originates from the market's internal mechanics—often amplified by automation, liquidity gaps, or feedback loops. These are often fast-moving and unpredictable, with effects that ripple through various asset classes.

Key Examples:

- **Flash Crashes:**

Rapid, algorithm-driven selloffs due to erroneous orders, lack of liquidity, or stop-loss chain reactions.

Example: *The May 6, 2010, Flash Crash dropped the Dow nearly 1,000 points in minutes.*

- **Liquidity Crunches**:

When buyers or sellers dry up, causing massive price dislocations.

Example: *During COVID-19 in March 2020, bid-ask spreads in ETFs and options widened significantly as liquidity vanished.*

- **Algorithmic Feedback Loops:**

AI or algo-based systems can cause acceleration in one direction if multiple models react similarly to the same input.

Example: *Risk-parity funds triggering sell programs during volatility spikes.*

4. Geopolitical Catalysts

Geopolitical uncertainty often leads to broad-based risk aversion, supply chain disruption, and energy price volatility. These events can have global and long-term effects, depending on their nature and scope.

Key Examples:

- **Military Conflicts:**

Wars or invasions create risk-off sentiment and drive volatility in defense, oil, and gold.

Example: *Russia's invasion of Ukraine in 2022 caused massive spikes in oil prices and defense stocks, along with a global market selloff.*

- **Global Health Crises:**

Pandemics or health emergencies disrupt global trade, demand, and productivity.

Example: *The onset of COVID-19 caused the fastest bear market in history (S&P 500 dropped 34% in 33 days).*

- **Trade Wars and Tariffs:**

Rising tensions between major economies (e.g., U.S.-China) can derail global supply chains and corporate profits.

Example: *The 2018–2019 U.S.-China trade war caused volatility surges every time tariffs were proposed, delayed, or escalated.*

- **Natural Disasters:**

Earthquakes, hurricanes, or wildfires can affect commodity prices, insurance stocks, and GDP outlooks.

Example: *Hurricane Katrina disrupted U.S. energy infrastructure, and oil futures soared.*

5. The Common Result: Uncertainty and Risk Repricing

Across all categories, these catalysts result in a similar chain of reactions:

1. **Spike in Implied Volatility (IV):** Options become more expensive as uncertainty rises.
2. **Wider Bid-Ask Spreads:** Liquidity providers step back, increasing slippage risk.
3. **Hedging Demand Rises:** Traders pile into puts, VIX products, or inversely correlated assets.
4. **Higher Correlation Across Assets:** Market movement becomes more uniform (everything moves together).

For options traders, recognizing these catalysts not only allows better preparation—but also opens the door to strategic opportunities. Volatility is not merely something to survive; it's often the engine of campaign profitability.

D. Core Volatility Indicators: VIX, IV Rank, Expected Move Models

Measuring volatility is essential for successful options trading. These indicators help traders assess the cost of option premiums, anticipate risk, and select the most effective strategy in various market environments. Whether managing an existing position or planning a new one, understanding how these tools function is critical to aligning your trades with market expectations.

1. VIX – The CBOE Volatility Index

Commonly known as the "fear gauge," the VIX measures the 30-day implied volatility of the S&P 500 Index (SPX) options. It reflects investor expectations for near-term market movement, based on the prices of out-of-the-money options.

Key Characteristics:

- **VIX is mean-reverting:** It tends to return to its average over time, which makes extreme values highly actionable for contrarian traders.

- **A rising VIX** indicates increasing demand for protection (typically via put options), often during market stress.
- **A falling VIX** suggests complacency or a more stable market environment.

Example:

- In early 2020, during the COVID crash, the VIX soared to nearly 85, signaling extreme panic. This was a massive rise from its long-term average of around 15–20.
- A trader seeing VIX spike from 20 to 35 might choose to reduce size, hedge directional trades, or consider strategies like iron condors or calendar spreads to take advantage of inflated option premiums.

2. IV Rank – Contextualizing Implied Volatility

IV Rank compares the current implied volatility (IV) of an underlying asset to its range over the past 12 months. This tool is especially valuable because IV in isolation can be misleading. A stock with 50% IV might sound high—but if it's been as high as 80% and as low as 10%, that 50% sits right in the middle.

- **Formula Example:**
- **Current IV:** 40%
- **Lowest IV (12 months):** 20%
- **Highest IV (12 months):** 60%
- **IV Rank = (40 - 20) / (60 - 20) × 100 = 50%**

So, a 50% IV Rank means IV is mid-range compared to its past levels.

Interpretation:

- IV Rank of 80% or higher → Options are expensive relative to their historical range.
- IV Rank of 20% or lower → Options are cheap, possibly underpricing upcoming movement.

3. Expected Move Models – Quantifying the Probable Range

Expected move (EM) is the market's consensus estimate for how much a stock or index is expected to move over a specific time frame. It is derived from option prices, typically from the ATM straddle, and represents a one-standard-deviation range.

Formula (simplified):

Expected Move = ATM Call Premium + ATM Put Premium

This tells traders the range within which the market expects the stock to trade, with roughly 68% probability over the selected expiration.

Example:

- SPY is trading at $420.
- ATM Call = $5.10, ATM Put = $4.90
- Expected move for the week = $10 (5.10 + 4.90)
- Traders expect SPY to stay within $410 to $430 over the next 5 trading days.

How These Indicators Work Together

Scenario	VIX	IV Rank	Expected Move	Strategic Consideration
Market Calm	Low (<15)	Low (<25%)	Narrow	Consider long premium (e.g., debit spreads)
Event Risk (Earnings/Fed)	Rising	Medium-High (60–90%)	Wide	Consider selling premium (e.g., calendars, condors)
Panic Selloff	Spiking (>35)	Very High (90%+)	Extremely Wide	Reduce position size, consider hedging or contrarian fades

Understanding volatility through tools like VIX, IV Rank, and Expected Move models allows traders to be proactive instead of reactive. These indicators not only guide strategy selection, but also help define realistic risk parameters, premium expectations, and probability zones.

Volatility isn't just a market condition—it's a tradeable feature. Mastering these tools gives you the edge to turn chaos into calculated opportunity.

Volatility indicators are not just technical curiosities—they are strategic tools. Mastering VIX, IV Rank, and Expected Move Models helps traders determine when to sell or buy premium, estimate risk boundaries, and align trades with market sentiment.

In volatile markets, success depends not just on what direction you trade—but on how you interpret volatility. With these tools, you'll be positioned to turn uncertainty into a strategic advantage.

E. How Volatility Affects Option Pricing, Spreads, and Trade Opportunity

Volatility is a core pricing input in options markets, and its fluctuations can create both opportunities and risks for traders. Understanding how implied volatility (IV) interacts with key components of the options chain can significantly enhance decision-making, especially in the context of multi-leg campaign strategies.

1. Option Premiums

Implied volatility is a direct factor in option pricing—higher IV inflates the time value portion of an option, increasing premiums, particularly for out-of-the-money (OTM) and at-the-money (ATM) contracts.

- **Higher IV → Higher Option Prices:**
    - When markets anticipate large moves (e.g., before earnings), IV increases, and option premiums rise.
    - This benefits premium sellers, as more credit can be collected.

Example: Before an EV Manufacturing stock's earnings, IV might spike from 50% to 75%. A weekly 10-point-wide iron condor that usually collects $1.20 might now collect $2.50 or more, significantly improving reward potential—if the stock stays within the expected range.

2. Bid-Ask Spreads

In volatile conditions, market makers face more uncertainty and hedge risk more conservatively. This leads to wider bid-ask spreads, which can:

- Increase execution costs (slippage)
- Make active trading or adjusting less efficient
- Require limit orders and greater patience

Example: In calm conditions, a mature software stock's weekly ATM call might have a bid-ask spread of $2.00 x $2.05. During a market-wide selloff, that same contract might spread to $1.70 x $2.20. For campaign traders scaling in or adjusting, this can eat into profits or create fill delays.

3. Probability Models and Expected Moves

Volatility also affects probability distributions. Higher IV leads to wider expected moves, reducing the statistical probability that a stock will stay in a defined range.

This directly impacts the profitability of strategies like condors, butterflies, and calendars—and encourages campaign traders to:

- Select wider strike spacing
- Use higher credit targets
- Be more proactive with adjustments

Example: If a smartphone stock has a weekly expected move of $4 under normal IV, a trader might use a short strangle with $5 wings. But if IV rises and the expected move increases to $7, the same structure would need $8–$10 wings—or be replaced with a different strategy entirely (e.g., a broken-wing butterfly).

F. Impact on Campaign Trading

For campaign-style traders, volatility introduces a double-edged sword:

- Higher Rewards: More premium can be collected, and directional trades can pay out faster.
- Higher Risk: Position values can fluctuate more wildly, requiring more vigilant management.

Effective campaign trading during high volatility involves:

- Strategic entry timing (e.g., entering after a volatility spike, not during it)
- Adjustments based on IV contraction or expansion
- Using tools like delta, gamma, and expected move models to guide each phase of the campaign

Pro Tip: Traders can use elevated volatility to initiate multi-phase positions (e.g., short puts followed by diagonal spreads) and allow IV contraction to create profit even in sideways price movement.

Volatility affects:

Factor	Effect of Rising IV	Trading Implications
Option Premiums	Increases	Good for sellers, expensive for buyers
Bid-Ask Spreads	Widens	Requires precision in order placement
Expected Move	Expands	Reduces likelihood of narrow-range strategies succeeding

For campaign traders, volatility is a powerful ally—but it demands precision, flexibility, and disciplined trade management. Knowing how volatility alters every layer of the options chain allows traders to construct more effective, profitable campaigns—no matter how chaotic the market appears.

G. Why Volatility Can Be a Strategic Advantage for the Prepared Trader

To the average investor, volatility is synonymous with risk. It conjures fear, erratic price movement, and the potential for loss. But for the **campaign trader,** volatility is an **engine of opportunity**—a dynamic force that enables **premium-rich trades, adaptive strategies, and accelerated returns.**

1. Volatility Creates Mispricings and Dislocations

Rapid market moves often cause temporary dislocations between stock price and option valuation. Market makers adjust pricing models on the fly, often creating mispriced volatility **surfaces** and **IV skews.**

Example: During a news-driven selloff, short-dated puts on SPY may become overly expensive relative to longer-dated puts. A trader can exploit this by entering a **put diagonal spread**—buying longer-dated puts and selling inflated short-term options, profiting from the decay and IV contraction.

2. Volatility Enriches Premium

Higher IV boosts the time value of options across the board. For traders who are equipped with **risk-defined structures**, this translates into higher credit received for the same amount of margin or buying power.

Example: A 10-point wide iron condor on a SmartPhone manufacturing stock may yield $1.00 during calm conditions but expand to $2.40 during a volatility event. This increases the max reward while maintaining the same defined risk, **improving the reward-to-risk ratio.**

3. Enables Strategic Adjustments: Gamma Scalping and Rolls

Volatile markets enhance the profitability of **gamma scalping, calendar rolling**, and **delta-neutral hedging**. The price action needed to realize these strategies' full potential is driven by movement and reversion—both abundant in volatile environments.

Gamma Scalping Example: A trader long 5 ATM calls on XYZ at $100 with a delta of +250 and gamma of +50 can profit from both upside and downside moves by buying low and selling high through small stock adjustments. The increased volatility ensures there is enough motion to make scalping worthwhile. More on Gamma Scalping in Chapters 6, 7, and 8.

Rolling Example: A trader holding a short call that becomes threatened can roll it up and out, collecting additional premium due to elevated IV—offsetting unrealized loss while extending the campaign.

4. When Mapped Properly, Volatility Can Be Predicted

The key to exploiting volatility is not reacting, but **anticipating and preparing**. Tools like:

- **Decision Trees** (for if-then planning)
- **Scenario Testing** (using IV shifts and expected move projections)
- **Technical Triggers** (pivot zones, volatility squeezes, Bollinger Band expansions)

...allow the campaign trader to prepare adjustments before they're needed, and convert chaos into campaign structure.

Example: Using Bollinger Bands and IV Rank, a trader identifies compression in a semiconductor stock. When the price breaks out and IV expands, the trader initiates a calendar spread—timing the expansion for maximum edge.

Strategic Benefits for Campaign Traders

Benefit	Volatility Impact	Trade Opportunity
Higher Option Premiums	Increases credit collected for spreads	Iron condors, short strangles
Price Dislocation	Misaligned IV skews and under/overpriced contracts	Diagonals, broken-wing butterflies
Adjustments Become Viable	Price movement creates profitable rolling windows	Roll calls/puts, gamma scalping
Greater Range Opportunities	Wider expected moves create more structured trades	Multi-leg campaigns with layered entries

For campaign traders, volatility is not something to fear—but to **prepare for, plan around, and profit from**. By using volatility-focused tools, disciplined adjustment planning, and proactive scenario modeling, a trader turns uncertainty into strategic clarity.

Volatility is motion. And motion, when harnessed properly, becomes momentum.

Campaign traders don't survive volatility—they thrive in it.

In this book, you'll learn how to structure and manage option positions in ways that embrace volatility instead of resisting it. The chapters ahead will arm you with tools, strategies, and real-world insights to master the craft of campaign trading in a fast-moving world.

You'll move beyond static strategies and reactive trades. Instead, you'll be equipped to build **multi-phase, adaptable positions** that evolve as the market changes—whether volatility is rising, falling, or spiking unpredictably. This book emphasizes **systematic flexibility:** how to enter trades with purpose, adjust them intelligently, and respond decisively to market catalysts.

You'll explore powerful concepts like:

- Using volatility metrics to guide strategy selection
- Crafting delta- and gamma-aware structures for sustained advantage
- Practicing campaign-style management that balances opportunity with risk control

Each chapter is filled with **visuals, case studies, and step-by-step tactics** that demystify complex spreads and turn theory into action. Whether you're managing a single iron condor or a layered diagonal portfolio, the skills in this book will help you thrive in the one constant of the modern market: **volatility**.

Welcome to the playbook for traders who don't just react to change—they build their edge on it.

Chapter: 2

Option Greeks in a Volatile World

In campaign trading, where trades are structured with foresight and refined through adjustment, understanding how options respond to changing market conditions is essential. This is where the option Greeks come into play. In volatile markets, the Greeks aren't just theoretical measures—they're your roadmap to dynamic risk control and strategic opportunity.

In this book, you'll learn how to structure and manage option positions in ways that embrace volatility instead of resisting it. Volatility isn't an obstacle—it's the fuel that powers strategic advantage when approached with the right mindset and tools. The chapters ahead will arm you with tools, strategies, and real-world insights to master the craft of campaign trading in a fast-moving world.

You'll move beyond static, one-size-fits-all strategies and reactionary trades that rely on luck. Instead, you'll be equipped to build multi-phase, adaptable positions that evolve as the market changes—whether volatility is rising, falling, or spiking unpredictably. This book emphasizes systematic flexibility: how to enter trades with purpose, adjust them intelligently, and respond decisively to market catalysts.

You'll explore powerful concepts like:

Using volatility metrics to guide strategy selection

You'll learn to interpret tools like VIX, IV Rank, and expected move models to align strategy choice with market conditions. For example, when IV Rank is above 80%, you'll know when it's ideal to sell premium through iron condors or calendar spreads. When IV is low, you'll learn how to capitalize on expansion with long debit spreads or straddles.

Crafting delta- and gamma-aware structures for sustained advantage

Understand how to balance directional exposure (delta) and reactivity to price movement (gamma). For example, you'll learn how gamma scalping works through dynamic delta-neutral hedging using long options and stock adjustments—generating profits from price swings without needing to predict direction.

Building adjustment paths for scenario planning

Instead of hoping your trade works out, you'll be guided to anticipate changes: "If the stock moves up, I roll the short call. If volatility contracts, I close half the position." Campaign trading is about proactive management.

Practicing campaign-style management that balances opportunity with risk control

You'll learn how to scale in and out, stagger expirations to maximize theta decay, and adjust your trading approach. Risk control comes not from avoidance—but from having a framework for what to do before, during, and after-market events.

Each chapter is filled with visuals, case studies, and step-by-step tactics that demystify complex spreads and turn theory into action. You'll work through examples like:

- Managing pivots during a surprise CPI report
- Gamma Scalping to make money even when the market is not trending, and rolling a gamma scalping campaign across volatile earnings weeks
- Deep in the Money Calls and Puts for short-term profits

Whether you're managing a single position or building a diversified portfolio of layered option spreads, the skills in this book will help you thrive in the one constant of the modern market: volatility.

A. Delta, Gamma, Theta, Vega, and Rho Explained Through Volatility

Understanding the Greeks is essential for campaign traders operating in volatile markets. These metrics allow you to decode how your option positions behave as prices shift, time passes, and volatility changes. In high-volatility environments, these sensitivities become more pronounced—turning the Greeks into powerful tools for prediction, protection, and profit.

Delta (Δ): Directional Exposure

Delta measures how much an option's price is expected to change for every $1 move in the price of the underlying asset. A delta of 0.50 suggests the option will gain or lose approximately $0.50 for every $1 move in the stock.

- Call options have positive delta (0 to 1.0); put options have negative delta (-1.0 to 0).
- Delta also acts as a proxy for the probability of expiring in-the-money.

Example: A near-the-money Smart Phone manufacturing stock call with a 0.55 delta will gain about $55 per contract for every $1 the stock rises.

In Volatility:

- Delta becomes more sensitive near expiration and near-the-money, especially when volatility is rising.
- Campaign traders use delta to construct directional biases, or build delta-neutral spreads (e.g., calendars or iron condors) that can evolve with market conditions.
- Delta hedging (through buying or selling stock) becomes more dynamic during volatility swings.

Gamma (Γ): Delta's Sensitivity to Price Movement

Gamma measures how much delta will change for each $1 move in the underlying asset.

- Gamma is highest for at-the-money options with short expiration.
- It tells traders how quickly they need to adjust to maintain a delta-neutral stance.

Example: A gamma of 0.05 means delta will increase or decrease by 0.05 for each $1 move in the stock.

In Volatility:

- When price moves rapidly, delta can swing quickly, requiring constant rebalancing.
- Gamma is essential in gamma scalping strategies—where traders use long options to capture profits through small stock moves.
- Around events (earnings, FOMC), gamma spikes, making positions more reactive but also more fragile.

Theta (Θ): Time Decay

Theta represents the rate of time decay of an option—how much value it loses daily as expiration approaches.

- Theta increases the closer an option is to expiration.
- Long options suffer from theta decay; short options benefit from it.

Example: A theta of -0.10 means the option loses $10 in value each day (per contract).

In Volatility:

- High IV often inflates premiums—but if the stock doesn't move, theta eats away at long premium positions.
- Traders must balance theta risk vs. movement potential. For example, long straddles require movement to offset theta erosion.
- Campaign traders often manage theta decay by layering calendars, diagonals, and roll techniques.

Vega (ν): Sensitivity to Volatility Changes

Vega measures how much an option's price will change for a 1% change in implied volatility (IV).

- Vega is higher for longer-dated and at-the-money options.
- A rise in IV inflates option prices; a drop deflates them.

Example: A vega of 0.12 means the option will gain $12 per contract for every 1% increase in IV.

In Volatility:

- Vega is your best friend or worst enemy during IV spikes around events.
- Calendars, diagonals, and long straddles benefit from rising vega.
- Credit spreads and short options suffer from sudden IV expansion—hence the importance of managing vega exposure.

Rho (ϱ): Interest Rate Sensitivity

Rho measures how much an option's price changes with a 1% change in interest rates.

- Rho is usually negligible for short-term trades.
- Longer-dated options (LEAPS) are more affected by rho.

Example: A rho of 0.06 means the option gains $6 per contract for every 1% rise in interest rates.

In Volatility:

- While less impactful day-to-day, campaign traders using long-dated diagonals or LEAPS may account for changing rate environments.
- For example, in a rising-rate regime, call options tend to increase slightly in value, while puts may lose some.

Summary Table: Greek Behavior in Volatility

Greek	Measures	Volatility Impact	Strategy Consideration
Delta	Price sensitivity	Becomes unstable near events and near ATM	Monitor directional exposure and hedge frequently
Gamma	Rate of delta change	Increases around ATM, short expiry	Use for scalping and aggressive rebalancing
Theta	Time decay	Accelerates if price stalls	Beware of long options, benefit with short
Vega	IV sensitivity	Higher in longer-dated options	Align with IV expectations and event planning
Rho	Interest rate sensitivity	Minor in short-term, relevant in LEAPS	Consider long-term structures

Understanding how each Greek reacts to volatility—and how they interact—empowers campaign traders to design trades that adapt and evolve. Mastering the Greeks is essential for thriving in a world where volatility is constant, not an exception.

B. Interactions Between Greeks During Volatility Spikes and Contractions

The option Greeks—Delta, Gamma, Theta, Vega, and Rho—do not operate in isolation. They are interconnected variables that respond collectively to changes in market volatility, price action, and time decay. For campaign traders, understanding these interactions is critical to anticipating risk and timing adjustments before positions deteriorate.

1. During Volatility Spikes

Volatility spikes often occur due to earnings announcements, the release of macroeconomic data, geopolitical tensions, or sudden shifts in market sentiment. These events create sharp price movements and emotional trading responses, which ripple across the Greeks.

What Happens:

- Delta becomes more erratic as Gamma increases. This is most noticeable in at-the-money (ATM) options near expiration, where small price moves in the underlying lead to large swings in Delta.
- Gamma spikes in near-term, ATM options, causing hedging requirements to rise. Traders may need to buy/sell shares frequently to stay delta-neutral.
- Theta slows temporarily because IV expansion inflates premiums, delaying time decay. However, this is a false cushion—as decay returns with force when IV contracts.
- Vega increases sharply, making long premium positions (e.g., long calls, straddles, calendars) temporarily more profitable.

Example: Suppose you hold a short strangle on an EV manufacturing stock during an unexpected volatility surge (IV rises from 40% to 70%).

- The Vega exposure of your short options causes large mark-to-market losses.
- Gamma spikes at the short strikes, making delta adjustments more reactive.
- You must decide whether to roll or hedge aggressively to manage the exposure.

2. During Volatility Contractions

After a high-impact event passes—such as post-earnings, Fed announcements, or geopolitical resolution—markets often enter a volatility contraction phase. This is where risk transitions from price movement to time decay and volatility normalization.

What Happens:

- Vega collapses, resulting in what traders call an IV crush. Long options lose value quickly, especially those purchased before the event.
- Theta accelerates, particularly in near-term, OTM options that now have lower IV and little directional potential.
- Gamma decreases, causing Delta to stabilize. This reduces the urgency for hedging adjustments, especially in spreads or calendars.

Example: You enter a long calendar spread on a Streaming Company's stock just before earnings, expecting a volatility spike. After earnings:

- Implied volatility drops from 90% to 45%.
- The short front-month option loses value quickly (good for you), but your long leg also drops in price due to the Vega crush.
- If the stock remains near the short strike, the calendar still profits—but only if you anticipated and priced the IV drop correctly.

The Greek Chain Reaction

Event	Delta	Gamma	Theta	Vega
Volatility Spike	Erratic (swings)	Sharp Increase	Slows temporarily	Increases sharply
Volatility Drop	Stabilizes	Declines	Speeds up	Collapses

3. Strategic Takeaways for Campaign Traders

- Anticipate, don't react. Use volatility forecasts (IV Rank, earnings calendars, Fed timelines) to structure positions based on expected Greek behavior.

- Adjust proactively. During spikes, widen spreads, hedge delta more frequently, or reduce size. Post-event, close long premium trades early or reconfigure into lower-Vega positions.
- Use structure to absorb shock. Layered positions (e.g., batmans-double diagonals, broken-wing butterflies) naturally buffer against Greek volatility by spreading risk across time and strikes.

Campaign traders who internalize the interactions between Greeks are able to manage risk dynamically, adjust more effectively, and stay ahead of the market's twists—not just survive them.

Mastering these relationships is what transforms a good options trader into a great one.

C. Identifying Favorable Greek Profiles for Volatile Market Strategies

Every options strategy is defined by its unique combination of Greek exposures—Delta, Gamma, Vega, and Theta. In volatile markets, the trader's edge lies in deliberately selecting a Greek profile that matches their outlook on price direction, volatility movement, and time decay dynamics.

Here's how different strategies stack up across the Greeks, and how campaign traders can use this insight to their advantage:

Strategy	Delta	Gamma	Vega	Theta
Long Straddle/Strangle	Neutral	High	Long	Negative
Short Iron Condor	Neutral	Low	Short	Positive
Calendar Spread	Slightly Directional	Medium	Long	Neutral / Negative
Diagonal Spread	Directional	Medium	Long	Variable
Gamma Scalping	Neutral	High	Long	Varies

Matching Greek Profiles to Market Conditions

1. Explosive Movement Expected? Seek High Gamma and Long Vega

If you expect a large price move, such as during earnings, Fed announcements, or macro shocks, prioritize:

- High Gamma: Enables quick delta adjustment and responsive profit capture.
- Long Vega: Benefits from increased IV before or during the event.

Examples:

- Long straddles/strangles around Smart-Phone manufacturing stock's earnings
- Gamma scalping using long ATM calls or puts in SPY before a rate decision

Tip: Be prepared to manage Theta decay aggressively if the move doesn't materialize quickly.

2. Sideways Market with High IV? Use Short Vega, Positive Theta

If the market is elevated in implied volatility but expected to trade in a range:

- **Short Vega:** Take advantage of inflated premiums.
- **Positive Theta:** Profit daily from time decay.

Examples:

- Iron condors on indexes like RUT or SPX in pre-holiday sessions
- Short strangles on high-IV stocks post-earnings

Tip: Manage early if price approaches short strikes or IV unexpectedly expands.

3. Volatility Compression Play? Favor Calendars or Diagonals

If you expect volatility to compress gradually and price to hover near a key level:

- Long Vega: Ride IV contraction over time.
- Medium Gamma: Moderate sensitivity gives flexibility.
- Variable Theta: Can adjust based on strike distance and expiration skew.

Examples:

- Calendar spreads on a Semiconductor stock leading into a known earnings report.
- Diagonal call spread on an EV manufacturing stock with a bullish bias, but IV elevated

Tip: Diagonals offer greater delta control than calendars, allowing directional adjustments.

4. Day-to-Day Volatility Swings? Gamma Scalping Opportunities

If you anticipate whipsaw price action, gamma scalping is ideal:

- High Gamma: Lets you capitalize on back-and-forth price action.
- Neutral Delta: Allows focus on price movement, not direction.
- Variable Theta and Vega: Depends on the duration and contract selection.

Example:

- Buy 5 ATM calls on XYZ and dynamically hedge with stock as the price fluctuates.
- Sell shares when the price rises (delta increases), buy them back on a drop.

Tip: Works best in high-liquidity, high-volatility stocks.

Strategic Takeaway

Understanding and applying Greek profiles empowers campaign traders to:

- Align strategy with market conditions and volatility forecasts
- Pre-plan adjustment paths based on Greek sensitivity
- Capture edge by exploiting volatility behavior across time and price

The real skill lies not just in knowing what each Greek means—but in designing and selecting positions that express your thesis through a balance of risk, reward, and flexibility.

When your Greek profile is aligned with your volatility outlook, your trades are not only logical—they are structurally optimized to perform.

D. How to Use the Greeks to Measure, Adjust, and Control Risk

Campaign trading is all about intelligent adaptation—responding to shifting markets not with emotion, but with data-driven strategy. The option Greeks serve as the vital diagnostic tools that empower traders to measure exposure, evaluate scenarios, and implement timely adjustments.

Each Greek contributes a piece of the puzzle. Here's how campaign traders apply them throughout the life of a trade:

1. Adjusting Delta: Managing Directional Exposure

Delta reveals how much your position will change in value for each $1 move in the underlying asset. If a trade becomes too directional—perhaps due to an unexpected price surge—the trader may need to neutralize risk.

How to Adjust:

- Roll strikes closer or further from the money
- Add an opposite-direction leg (e.g., buy a put to reduce net positive delta)
- Hedge with stock in small lots to return to delta-neutral

Example: You're running a bullish diagonal spread on XYZ stock. The stock jumps 5%, increasing your net delta from +60 to +150. To reduce directional risk:

- Sell stock to bring delta closer to +75
- Or roll the short call strike higher to reduce exposure and collect more credit

2. Controlling Gamma Risk: Reactivity Management

Gamma tells you how quickly delta will change. High gamma = high sensitivity, especially around expiration or with ATM options.

How to Adjust:

- Reduce size in short-term ATM options before major events
- Close or roll positions that become too reactive
- Add wider spreads to dampen gamma exposure

Example: You're long 5 near-the-money weekly calls on XYZ stock heading into earnings. Gamma is high, meaning a small move could drastically change your delta. To avoid overreacting:

- Roll to next week's expiration for smoother gamma
- Or close part of the position and replace it with longer-dated options

3. Managing Theta: Dealing with Time Decay

Theta measures how much your option's value erodes daily. While useful for premium sellers, it's dangerous for long positions in a non-moving market.

How to Adjust:

- Close legs that are too far OTM and bleeding value
- Shift toward longer expirations for less decay
- Transition into spreads that mitigate net theta loss

Example: You're holding a long straddle on SPY. After two days of sideways action, your theta exposure is -30. Rather than holding and hoping:

- Sell one leg to convert it to a directional call or put

- Or roll to a calendar to benefit from future IV shifts

4. Monitoring Vega: Anticipating IV Changes

Vega represents your sensitivity to changes in implied volatility. In volatile markets, timing IV exposure is everything.

How to Adjust:

- Reduce long vega positions before known IV crush events (e.g., earnings)
- Use spreads with offsetting vega (e.g., calendars, diagonals)
- Scale into positions after IV contraction for better pricing

Example: You've opened a long calendar spread on XYZ stock ahead of earnings, expecting a volatility bump. Once earnings pass and IV collapses:

- Your long leg loses value sharply
- The short leg expires worthless
- Consider closing or rolling the long leg into another structure

5. Putting It All Together: Campaign Execution in Practice

Advanced traders don't just check the Greeks—they proactively anticipate adjustments based on possible changes in delta, gamma, theta, and vega that will influence their trade.

Summary Table: Using Greeks to Adjust and Control Risk

Greek	When to Adjust	How to Adjust
Delta	Too directional / unbalanced exposure	Roll strikes, hedge with stock, adjust leg ratios
Gamma	Near expiration / high reactivity	Shift expirations, close/restructure ATM trades
Theta	Stalled market / high decay on long premium	Roll or close legs, switch to longer expirations
Vega	Pre-event spikes or post-event IV crush	Reduce long vega, switch to defined-risk spreads

Successful campaign traders treat the Greeks like the dashboard of a high-performance vehicle. Each dial tells you how the trade will behave—before the road turns. By learning to read and respond to them, you gain the control needed to thrive in any volatility environment.

Let's review an AI Generated Response concerning how Option Greeks may change based on volatile markets moves:

Prompt:

During a volatile market period driven by global economic turmoil and trade policy disruptions, describe how option put Greeks may react during a significant 3-day market pullback and how they would be expected to react during a quick recover from this drop. Provide examples and explain the theory behind your conclusions.

Response with ChatGPT:

During a ***volatile market period****—especially one driven by global economic turmoil and trade policy disruptions—****option put Greeks*** *exhibit dramatic and often interconnected changes. These shifts are a result of rapid changes in price, volatility, and market sentiment. Here's how the primary Greeks for put options typically react over the course of a* ***3-day market pullback and a quick recovery:***

During a 3-Day Market Pullback: Greek Reactions for Put Options

1. Delta (Δ): Increases Toward -1

- **Theory:** *Put delta measures the rate of change of the put option's value as the underlying declines. For puts, delta is negative and grows more negative as the underlying price drops.*
- **Example:** *Suppose a trader owns a 100 strike put on XYZ, currently at $102 with delta = -0.40. As the stock drops to $95, delta may deepen to -0.65 or lower.*
- **Interpretation:** *The put behaves more like a short stock as delta approaches -1, increasing its sensitivity to price drops.*

2. Gamma (Γ): Increases Then Decreases

- **Theory:** *Gamma measures the rate of change in delta. Gamma is highest at-the-money and increases as the option approaches ATM territory from OTM.*
- **Example:** *A 100 strike put, originally OTM, becomes ATM on day 2 as the stock falls to $100, causing gamma to spike. If the stock drops further to $95 (deep ITM), gamma declines again.*
- **Interpretation:** *The most dynamic delta changes (and thus the most gamma exposure) happen mid-pullback. Traders need to hedge frequently during this window.*

3. Theta (Θ): Becomes Less Negative

- **Theory:** *Theta measures time decay. In high IV conditions and when a put moves ITM, theta erosion slows because intrinsic value increases.*
- **Example:** *A put that was decaying at $-0.05/day might reduce to $-0.02/day as it gains value from the drop in stock price.*
- **Interpretation:** *The pullback slows theta loss, making longer-dated puts more attractive during downturns.*

4. Vega (ν): Increases—IV Spikes

- **Theory:** *Vega measures sensitivity to implied volatility. During market drops, IV typically rises due to panic and demand for protection.*
- **Example:** *If IV rises from 25% to 35%, the value of the put option*

jumps substantially—even independent of price movement.

- **Interpretation:** *This "volatility pop" boosts put premium, making them more profitable during pullbacks.*

During a Quick Market Recovery: Greek Reactions for Put Options

1. Delta: Moves Closer to 0

- *As the stock recovers, ITM puts move back toward OTM or ATM, reducing delta magnitude (e.g., from -0.70 back to -0.30).*
- **Impact:** *Puts become less responsive to price increases; losses accelerate.*

2. Gamma: Increases Briefly Near ATM, Then Falls

- *If the recovery pushes the stock near the put strike, gamma spikes again—this time working against the trader holding puts.*
- **Risk:** *Traders short gamma during rebounds faces rapid losses if they're unhedged.*

3. Theta: Increases—Decay Accelerates

- *As IV drops and the option loses intrinsic value, theta decay intensifies.*
- *Effect: Short-dated puts can lose value rapidly even if the price doesn't rise significantly.*

4. Vega: Contracts Significantly

- *As fear subsides, IV falls (volatility crush).*
- **Example:** *IV drops from 35% back to 25%, reducing put premium.*
- **Impact:** *Long puts lose value even if the stock remains flat or declines modestly.*

Example Timeline: 100 Strike Put on XYZ Stock

Day	*XYZ Price*	*Delta*	*Gamma*	*Vega*	*IV (%)*	*Option Value (est.)*
0	*$102*	*-0.35*	*0.05*	*0.10*	*25%*	*$2.00*
1	*$100*	*-0.50*	*0.08*	*0.12*	*30%*	*$3.25*
2	*$95*	*-0.70*	*0.04*	*0.14*	*35%*	*$6.75*
3	*$100*	*-0.45*	*0.06*	*0.10*	*27%*	*$3.00*
4	*$103*	*-0.25*	*0.03*	*0.07*	*22%*	*$1.25*

Conclusion

Understanding Greek dynamics in volatile markets allows traders to:

- ***Buy puts before fear fully enters the market*** *(capitalize on IV expansion).*
- ***Scalp or close positions as gamma peaks*** *to lock in profits.*
- ***Avoid holding long puts into rebounds,*** *as IV crush and falling delta cause rapid losses.*

In volatile environments, it's not just price direction that matters—but how fast and how far Greeks move in response. Gamma scalpers, spread traders, and directional put buyers must adjust their strategies in real time to exploit or defend against these shifts.

Final Thoughts

In a volatile world, mastering the Greeks transforms a trader from reactive to proactive. It's not about avoiding risk—it's about engineering positions that breathe with the market and evolve as conditions shift. Just as a pilot adjusts altitude, airspeed, and heading based on real-time weather data, the campaign trader adjusts delta, gamma, theta, and vega in response to changing market forces.

The true edge lies in your ability to interpret these metrics not as static numbers, but as dynamic signals guiding structure, sizing, and timing. By integrating the Greeks into every stage of the trade—

entry, management, and exit—you move from guesswork to precision.

When you understand:

- How delta expands and contracts with price movement
- How gamma creates opportunity and risk in rapid markets
- How theta decays value unless managed correctly
- How vega rewards or punishes exposure to volatility shifts

...you begin to trade with an architect's mindset. You no longer hope for favorable outcomes—you engineer them.

As you progress in this book, you'll see how these principles come to life through real trade structures, scenario planning, and campaign layering. The Greeks will become second nature, enabling you to proactively shape your trades instead of reacting after damage is done.

Coming Up Next: In the next chapter, we'll explore how to select the best strategies based on your volatility outlook, campaign goals, and trade profile. From directional momentum plays to non-directional income campaigns, you'll learn to map the market to the method—choosing the Greek profile that gives you the best edge in any environment.

Chapter: 3

Strategy Selection in Volatile Markets

Choosing the right strategy in a volatile market is like selecting the proper sail for the wind. The market's direction, intensity, and underlying tone all influence how we deploy capital. For campaign traders, strategy selection is not only about identifying a high-probability setup but also choosing an approach that allows for flexibility and adjustment as conditions evolve.

A. Framework for Strategy Selection: Directional vs. Neutral Bias

The first decision in strategy selection revolves around one foundational question: **What is your market bias?** Understanding whether you expect the underlying asset to move **up, down,** or sideways will guide the entire structure of your options position.

Step 1: Define Market Bias

1. Directional Bias

A directional bias means the trader expects a meaningful move in one direction—either bullish or bearish. This can be based on technical breakouts, fundamental catalysts, earnings reports, or macroeconomic forecasts.

Examples:

- **Bullish:** A trader expects an EV manufacturer to rally after a strong delivery report and enters a **bull call spread.**
- **Bearish:** A trader anticipates a pullback in a smartphone stock post-Fed announcement and buys a **put debit spread.**

Ideal Strategies:

- Long calls or puts
- Vertical debit spreads (bull call, bear put)
- Diagonal spreads with a directional tilt

2. Neutral Bias

A neutral bias reflects an expectation of sideways price movement or a range-bound consolidation. The trader believes the asset will stay within a defined window over a set time.

Examples:

- A trader notices that SPX has entered a range between 4100 and 4300 and sells an iron **condor** centered at 4200.
- With IV at historical highs, a trader enters a **calendar spread** on a large and mature software stock expecting the price to stall near $300.

Ideal Strategies:

- Short strangles or straddles (with caution and proper hedging)
- Iron condors
- Calendar or Batman spreads
- Broken-wing butterflies

In Volatile Markets: Match Bias with Volatility Edge

Volatility complicates—but also enhances—strategic opportunities. The key is to align strategy with bias and volatility expectations.

Directional Trades in Volatile Markets:

- Favor strategies that offer **defined risk and leveraged reward.**
- Use long options or narrow vertical spreads to capture moves while limiting loss.
- **Diagonals** are especially powerful when IV is expected to rise in the long leg while decaying in the short.

Example: If an AI semiconductor stock is trending and IV is climbing, a trader might buy a long-term call and sell a near-term OTM call, benefiting from the skew in IV and directional movement.

Neutral Trades in Volatile Markets:

- Favor strategies that **sell premium** and thrive on **IV contraction.**
- Use **wide iron condors** or **double calendars (possibly Batmans)** when IV is inflated and expected to drop post-event.
- Emphasize **theta decay** and position size management to weather unexpected moves.

Example: Before a known earnings event in an online retailer, IV spikes. A trader enters a double calendar spread around the expected move, aiming to capture decay and post-event IV drop.

Campaign Trader's Process:

1. **Start with Bias:** Where is the asset likely to go (or not go)?
2. **Overlay Volatility View:** Is IV high or low? Will it expand or contract?
3. **Assess Time Horizon:** Do you expect movement in hours, days, or weeks?
4. **Align Risk Tolerance:** How much capital are you willing to risk or allocate?
5. **Select Strategy & Strike Combo:** Choose spread width, expiration mismatch, and credit/debit structure.

Example Scenario:

- **Bias:** Neutral
- **Volatility:** High (expected to contract)
- **Strategy:** Iron condor
- **Strikes:** OTM legs set just outside 1-standard deviation
- **Management:** Adjust short strikes if delta shifts or IV re-expands unexpectedly

Key Takeaway: The right strategy is not just about choosing a spread—it's about choosing a bias and matching it to the environment. In volatile markets, this match determines whether you thrive on chaos or get caught off guard. With clear bias, volatility alignment, and adaptive structure, campaign traders can transform noise into profit.

B. Determining Profit Potential and Return

At Firebird, we are also very focused on how much you can make for what you invest in a trade. This table provides typical relative returns for the investment amount. Position selection is all relative to various factors such as:

- What are a trader's expectations? If your expectations are too high, you will be taking risks that are too high.
- Comfort level of a trader to manage a specific opening position. For instance, it would be much easier to manage a Covered Call than a multi-leg spread.
- Buying power required and whether your current portfolio is substantial enough to handle the possible adjustments required for an opening position if the market goes against you.

The following graphic shows the relative market bias vs the size of the trade required for various positions.

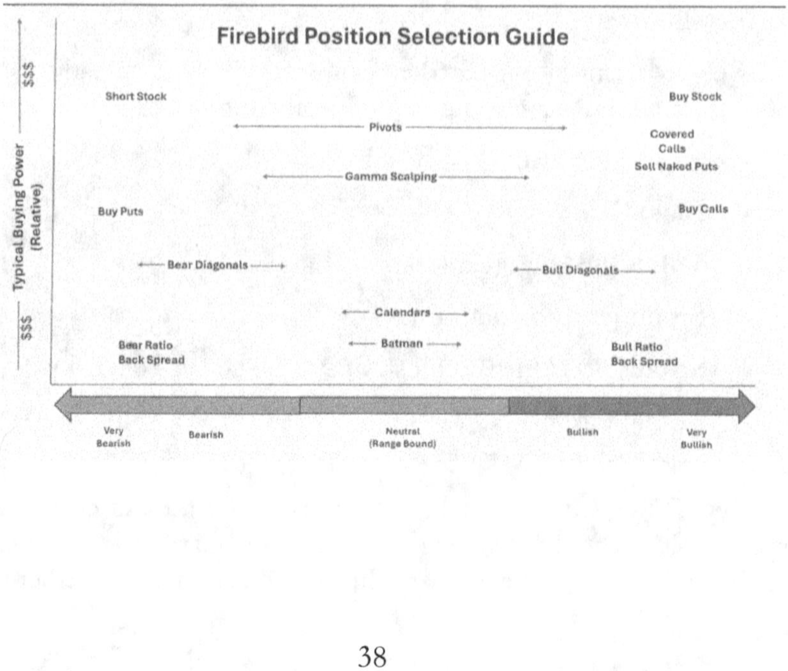

Also, remember that no matter what your market bias is, it could be wrong. A trader must consider his own record of selecting bias and decide how much he is willing to risk.

C. Matching Implied vs. Realized Volatility to Trade Design

Volatility is dynamic—not static—and understanding the interplay between **Implied Volatility (IV)** and **Realized Volatility (RV)** is critical for designing optimal options strategies. These two metrics offer different insights:

- **Implied Volatility (IV):** The market's expectations of future volatility, reflected in option pricing.
- **Realized Volatility (RV):** The actual historical movement of the underlying over a period of time.

The relationship between IV and RV highlights whether the market is **overpricing** or **underpricing** future risk. Campaign traders use this differential to **choose when to buy or sell premium,** determine **trade structure,** and inform **adjustment timing.**

When IV > RV: Sell Premium

When implied volatility exceeds historical volatility, it suggests that **options are expensive relative to actual market movement.** This is a signal to **sell premium**, since the market may be overstating risk.

Ideal Strategies:

- **Credit spreads:** Benefit from inflated option pricing while limiting risk.
- **Iron condors:** Use a wide range to capitalize on sideways movement and time decay.
- **Calendars/Diagonals:** Sell short-term options with elevated IV while holding longer-dated legs with lower IV.

Example: During earnings season, IV on a large mature software stock rises from 25% to 50%, while RV remains around 20%. A trader sells a short strangle or a narrow iron condor around the expected move range to collect a high premium and profit from post-event IV crush.

When IV < RV: Buy Premium

When IV is lower than RV, options may be **underpricing the actual market movement.** This is often a mispricing opportunity for buyers.

Ideal Strategies:

- **Long straddles/strangles:** Profit from larger-than-expected moves.
- **Long vertical spreads (debit):** Capture directional movement with limited cost.
- **Gamma scalping:** Take advantage of RV spikes using long ATM options.

Example: Suppose a smartphone company's stock's IV is 18% while the stock has been realizing 25% volatility due to macroeconomic turbulence. A trader buys a **long straddle** expecting continued whipsaws, aiming to profit from price swings and increasing IV.

Quantifying the IV/RV Relationship

Many trading platforms allow traders to compare IV and RV on the same chart. A few key metrics to watch:

- **IV Percentile or Rank:** High = options expensive; low = options cheap.
- **HV (20) vs. IV:** Compare 20-day historical volatility to current IV.
- **IV/RV Ratio:** Some traders use a ratio model to flag trade setups (e.g., IV is 1.5x RV).

Real-World Usage: A trader identifies that SPY has IV of 22% and RV of 14%—a high IV/RV ratio. They initiate an **iron condor** 1 standard deviation wide to capture premium decay post-news.

Campaign Trader's Takeaway

This IV vs. RV comparison becomes even more powerful when used in combination with:

- **Earnings calendars**
- **Expected move models**
- **Technical levels or pivot zones**

Campaign traders incorporate this insight at every stage:

- **Entry:** Identify setups where volatility dislocation offers an edge
- **Adjustment:** Shift structures based on changing IV/RV relationships
- **Exit:** Use mean-reversion in IV to time exits for optimal return

Rule of Thumb:

- **Sell premium** when IV is elevated—but only if the underlying is expected to behave calmly.
- **Buy premium** when IV is low—but only if you anticipate acceleration in price action or volatility.

Volatility isn't just noise—it's **pricing data embedded with market expectations.** Matching IV to RV allows campaign traders to design trades with the odds in their favor, capitalizing on both mispricing and market rhythm.

Prompt

What option positions or techniques are recommended to use in a volatile market that is expected to continue to be volatile?

Response with ChatGPT

In a volatile market that's expected to remain volatile, the key is to use strategies that benefit from or withstand large price swings, while managing risk. Here are the most recommended option techniques for that environment:

1. Straddles & Strangles (Volatility Plays)

Best for: *Expecting a big move but unsure of direction*

Long Straddle: *Buy a Call and a Put at the same strike price (ATM)*

Long Strangle: *Buy OTM Call and Put with wider strike separation*

Goal: *Capitalize on sharp price moves in either direction*

Risk: *Time decay and high implied volatility premiums*

Use near-term expirations and look for earnings or economic events to spark movement.

2. Iron Condors & Iron Butterflies (Volatility Sellers)

Best for: *Expecting volatility to contract after a spike*

Iron Condor: *Sell a wide call spread and put spread*

Iron Butterfly: *Sell ATM straddle and buy wings*

Goal: *Profit if price stays within a range*

Risk: *Breakouts in either direction*

Only use these when implied volatility is high and expected to drop.

3. Diagonal & Double Diagonal (Possibly Batman) Spreads

Best for: *Taking advantage of time decay and IV changes*

Diagonal Call/Put Spread: *Buy long-dated option, sell short-dated one*

Double Diagonal: *One Call and one Put diagonal (both OTM)*

Goal: *Gain from time decay and implied volatility differences*

Flexibility: *Can be adjusted to lean bullish or bearish*

Ideal for campaign-style adjustments and managing with technical levels.

4. Gamma Scalping (Advanced)

Best for: *Professional traders in high volatility*

Setup: *Long options (calls or puts), delta-hedged with stock*

Goal: *Profit from large intraday moves by adjusting delta*

Requirements: *Frequent monitoring, low execution cost*

Bonus: *Non-directional profits from price swings*

You "buy low, sell high" on the stock to offset option delta shifts.

5. Protective Puts / Collars (Hedging)

Best for: Holding stock and wanting downside protection

Protective Put: *Buy a put to hedge stock*

Collar: *Buy put + sell covered call*

Goal: *Limit loss while preserving upside (partially with collars)*

Perfect when managing a longer-term portfolio in turbulent times.

6. Skew & IV Rank Analysis Tools

Use tools to identify IV skew, IV rank, and high IV stocks to:

Pick optimal strategies (buying vs. selling volatility)

Time entries better (don't overpay for inflated options)

Firebird Pro Tip:

Combine TradeStation's RadarScreen with custom coded volatility filters (IV rank, delta skew, straddle break-evens) to scan for:

Best straddle setups

High gamma names for scalping

Iron condors with widest breakeven zones

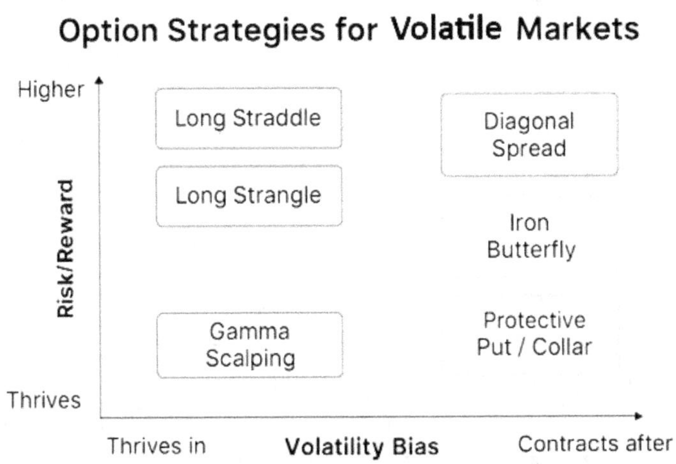

D. Scanning and Filtering Trades Using Technical + Volatility Tools

Identifying trades worth staging a campaign around requires more than scanning for price movement. The most effective setups arise from a blended approach—where technical indicators intersect with volatility insights to signal strategic opportunities. Campaign traders use sophisticated filters to narrow the universe of symbols into a list of high-conviction candidates that align with their bias, risk parameters, and trade structure.

Technical Indicators: Structure First

Technical analysis provides a framework for evaluating price behavior and predicting continuation or reversal.

Key Tools to Apply:

- **ADX (Average Directional Index):** Measures trend strength. A value above 25 suggests strong directionality—ideal for vertical or diagonal spreads.
- **RSI (Relative Strength Index):** Spot overbought/oversold extremes. RSI < 30 or > 70 can help time contrarian entries with long options or calendars.
- **Bollinger Band Width:** Indicates volatility compression or expansion. Narrow width = breakout potential; wide width = recent volatility spike.
- **Pivot Zones (Monthly/Weekly):** Serve as campaign reference levels to structure legs around.

Example: A large streaming company stock has RSI < 30 and ADX > 30 with price compressing into the lower Bollinger Band—trader enters a bullish diagonal call spread, expecting a rebound with rising IV.

Volatility Filters: Know the Pricing Environment

Even with a strong chart, mispriced volatility can sabotage a trade. Campaign traders filter based on IV metrics to find setups where options are cheap or rich relative to history.

Key Volatility Metrics:

- **IV Rank:** Where the current IV sits in its 12-month range. > 60% = high, < 30% = low.
- **IV Percentile:** Compares how often IV was lower historically—provides clearer context than raw IV.
- **IV Skew:** Measures differences between puts/calls or

near/far expirations. Useful for shaping calendars and diagonals.

Example: An EV manufacturing stock has an IV Rank of 85% with earnings 5 days out. A trader builds a double calendar with a wide strike selection to sell inflated near-term IV and hold long-term vega.

Options Metrics: Execution Matters

Once a setup looks viable, ensure the instrument is liquid, responsive, and cost-efficient.

Key Options Metrics:

- **Open Interest:** Confirms active interest. Avoid strikes with < 500 OI for liquid trading.
- **Bid/Ask Spread:** Look for narrow spreads (< $0.10) to minimize slippage.
- **Gamma Sensitivity:** Favor ATM options with high gamma for responsive delta hedging in gamma scalping or dynamic strategies.

Example: A large mature software company's 170 call has 8,000 OI and a $0.03 spread—suitable for building a calendar with short-term gamma risk management.

Automating the Screening Process

Manual scanning is very useful but somewhat slower. Campaign traders can also leverage platforms and tools to automate trade discovery and ensure consistent, bias-aligned filtering.

Automation Tools:

- **TradeStation RadarScreen:** Scan for technical and IV criteria across large watchlists or the entire universe of stocks.
- **EasyLanguage Scripts:** Create custom filters to flag setups based on volatility, trend, RSI, or skew.
- **ChatGPT + Volatility APIs:** Combine AI-powered logic with live market data to build watchlists and simulate forward-looking conditions.

Example Workflow:

1. **Use RadarScreen to scan for stocks with:**
   - o ADX > 25
   - o IV Rank > 70
   - o OI > 1,000 at ATM strikes

2. Run EasyLanguage script to flag those with tight spreads and weekly expirations.

3. Load results into a decision tree for strategy selection.

Strategic Edge: Focused Campaign Planning

Filtering with intent reduces noise. It helps campaign traders:

- Avoid chasing setups that aren't structurally sound.
- Focus energy on preparing adjustment scenarios in advance.
- Stay ahead of events where IV or technical shifts create opportunity.

By combining technical structure, volatility conditions, and execution quality, traders build a repeatable campaign discovery process that leads to higher win rates and better risk/reward setups. The goal isn't just to find trades—but to find the right trades, at the right time, with the right structure.

D. IV Skew and Timing Considerations for Entries and Adjustments

Volatility is not uniform across all strikes and expirations. **IV skew** reflects how implied volatility changes across the option chain:

- **Vertical Skew (Strike Skew):** OTM puts often carry more IV than ATM or OTM calls—especially in equities with downside fear.
- **Horizontal Skew (Term Structure):** Near-term options may have lower or higher IV than longer-dated ones, depending on event risk (earnings, Fed announcements).

Timing entries requires:

- Entering long premium trades **before** volatility expands

- Selling premium **after** a spike in IV, ideally when movement slows
- Rolling or adjusting legs when skew creates a pricing edge (e.g., sell higher IV, buy lower IV)

Campaign traders build into these moments, preparing alternate branches of the trade tree based on how skew and volatility develop over time.

Smart traders map IV skew onto decision trees. They:

- Plan legs that benefit from evolving skew
- Set alerts when skew widens abnormally
- Use skew to time legging into spreads instead of entering all at once

Decision Tree Branch Example:

- If IV flattens → roll into condor
- If near-term IV spikes → add calendar leg
- If back-month IV drops → convert diagonal into vertical

IV skew is more than an academic concept—it's a real-world edge for campaign traders. By:

- Selling rich legs
- Buying cheap legs
- Timing entries/adjustments around IV behavior

You position your campaign trades for better probability, smoother adjustments, and higher return consistency.

Train your eyes to see the skew—it's often where the edge hides.

Conclusion

Strategy selection in volatile markets is both art and science—a thoughtful mix of bias, edge, and adaptability. It begins by interpreting **what the market is offering**—in terms of trend, volatility regime, and pricing dislocations—and then identifying the **options structure that best exploits those conditions.**

Every campaign trade starts with a bias:

- Do you expect movement or consolidation?
- Will IV expand or contract?
- Is the skew providing a pricing advantage?

With these inputs, campaign traders construct strategies that reflect not only market expectations—but also include **mechanisms for adjustment and triggers for re-evaluation.**

By:

- Matching IV with expected volatility behavior (e.g., expanding, compressing, spiking)
- Filtering setups with technical and volatility-based tools
- Timing entries and managing risk with an eye toward skew and liquidity

...traders can design campaigns that **absorb volatility rather than resist it.**

Example Recap:

- **High IV & Neutral Bias:** Use iron condors, short straddles, or calendars around major earnings events
- **Low IV & Directional Bias:** Consider long vertical spreads or diagonals with strong technical support or Pivot at pivot points.
- **IV Spike + Reversion Expectation:** Sell rich legs and position for premium collapse with calendars or backspreads

Successful campaign trading isn't about making perfect calls—it's about building positions with the flexibility to evolve. Your strategy becomes a framework, not a fixed bet.

Chapter: 4

Trading Pivots: Direction and Decay

In volatile markets, successful campaign traders look for moments of structural opportunity—points where price, volatility, and time converge to create repeatable edge. These moments often occur at **trading pivots:** key zones where markets tend to turn, pause, or accelerate. This chapter explores how to define pivot points, why they matter, and how to deploy **diagonal** and **double diagonal spreads** based on starting with a long straddle or strangle to take full advantage of them. I call these Pivots to reflect the point of entry.

A. What Are Trading Pivots and How to Define Them

Trading pivots are **price zones where the market tends to reverse or consolidate** based on historical behavior. These levels are not just technical curiosities—they reflect institutional positioning, volume memory, and market psychology.

Traders can identify pivots using:

- **Historical high/low zones**
- **Previous support/resistance levels**
- **Volume profile peaks (high volume nodes)**
- **Fibonacci clusters and moving average confluence**
- **VWAP bands and anchored VWAP from key events**

A pivot doesn't need to be exact—it's a zone, not a price. Recognizing pivots allows traders to anticipate where volatility may increase, decrease, or shift direction.

Campaign traders use pivot zones to **stage entries, time adjustments,** and **layer trades** to maximize edge while managing risk.

Trading pivots are dynamic **price zones** where the market tends to **pause, reverse, or consolidate** based on historical trading behavior and institutional flow. Unlike static support/resistance lines, **pivots represent probabilistic battle zones**—areas of equilibrium or transition that can be leveraged by campaign traders to structure entries, exits, and adjustments.

These zones often emerge from repeated market memory, liquidity clustering, and **psychological thresholds** that institutions watch closely.

1. How to Identify Trading Pivots

Rather than relying on a single indicator, experienced traders **combine several tools** to identify meaningful pivot zones:

Historical Highs and Lows

- These are natural psychological reference points.
- Traders often place stops or limit orders near these levels.

Example: If a smartphones stock has bounced off $150 multiple times over the last 6 months, this area becomes a pivot for reversal or breakout.

Previous Support and Resistance Levels

- Classic technical zones where price has previously stalled.
- These areas often flip roles (support becomes resistance and vice versa).

Example: SPY previously resisted at 430 and broke out—430 may now act as a support pivot.

Volume Profile Peaks (High Volume Nodes)

- Price levels where high transaction volume occurred (consolidation zones).
- These indicate institutional positioning and liquidity comfort zones.

Example: Using a volume profile on an AI semiconductor stock reveals heavy volume between $420 and $435, creating a pivot band.

Fibonacci Clusters and Moving Average Confluence

- Fibonacci retracement levels often align with swing pivots.
- When major moving averages (20, 50, 200 EMA) converge near a Fib level, the area becomes of high interest.

Example: If a large mature software stock's 50-day MA and 38.2% retracement align near $290, that becomes a strong potential pivot.

VWAP Bands and Anchored VWAP from Key Events

- VWAP and anchored VWAP levels reflect institutional average cost.
- Anchoring VWAP to earnings, FOMC, or large-volume candles helps identify where institutions defend or reposition.

Example: Anchored VWAP from a Semiconductor stock's earnings candle aligns with a pullback zone = prime pivot for re-entry.

2. Campaign Trader's Use of Pivots

Campaign traders don't just observe pivots—**they build strategy branches around them:**

Entry Planning:

- Enter trades **just outside or just inside** pivot zones, depending on breakout/bounce probability.

Adjustment Zones:

- Use pivot zones as **inflection points** for rolling spreads, tightening condors, or converting positions.

Layering Trades:

- Stage diagonals or calendars at staggered strikes near a pivot range to **manage movement and capitalize on premium decay.**

Example Campaign Strategy:

- **Underlying:** QQQ
- **Bias:** Neutral to bullish
- **Pivot zone:** $360–$365 based on volume profile + VWAP confluence
- **Entry:** Long diagonal using a long 45-day $360 call and short 15-day $365 call

- **Adjustment Plan:** Roll short leg higher if price rallies through $365; roll lower if it stalls below $360

Pivots are **decision points**—not guarantees. They don't predict direction, but they help **frame risk, improve timing, and define opportunity zones.**

For campaign traders, pivot zones provide the **spatial structure** around which trades evolve, adjustments are staged, and outcomes are shaped.

In the next section, we'll explore how **diagonal and double diagonal spreads** thrive when positioned around these zones—delivering flexibility, premium edge, and a framework for campaign-style trade management.

B. Why Diagonal Spreads Are Ideal Near Pivot Zones

Diagonal spreads—buying one option and selling another with a different strike **and** expiration—offer flexibility, theta benefit, and directional bias.

In volatile environments, **diagonals shine** near pivots for several reasons:

- **Directional Flexibility:** Traders can lean slightly bullish or bearish while benefiting from time decay.
- **Skew Advantage:** Selling short-dated, high-IV options while holding longer-term, lower-IV options increases edge.
- **Adjustment-Friendly:** If price tests a pivot and holds or reverses, the structure can be rolled or scaled.

Campaign traders build diagonals around pivots to take advantage of **volatility clustering** and time-based value decay.

Diagonal spreads—constructed by **buying a longer-dated option** and **selling a shorter-dated option at a different strike**—are one of the most versatile structures in options trading. They combine elements of both calendar spreads and vertical spreads, making them a **strategic powerhouse near pivot zones**, especially in volatile markets.

Here's why campaign traders favor diagonals around pivots:

1. Directional Flexibility with Defined Risk

Pivots are areas of **indecision**—price may bounce, break out, or reverse. Diagonal spreads allow traders to express a **mild directional bias** (bullish or bearish) without committing to an outright directional bet.

Example: If SPY is testing a pivot zone at 420:

- A trader may buy a 45-day 415 call and sell a 15-day 420 call.
- If SPY rises slowly to 420, the short leg decays rapidly, allowing the trader to capture profit while the long leg retains value.

This setup allows you to **profit if the pivot holds or gets tested,** while managing exposure if price consolidates or drifts.

2. Skew Advantage and IV Edge

Implied volatility tends to **spike in shorter expirations**, especially around events like earnings, Fed decisions, or technical breakouts. Diagonal spreads let traders **sell high-IV short-term options** while **buying lower-IV long-term options**—creating a natural edge.

Example: A trader identifies a pivot zone on an EV manufacturing stock at $800 during an earnings week.

- Short-dated IV = 85%
- Longer-dated IV = 55%

The trader enters a diagonal by:

- Buying a 60-day 800 call
- Selling a 7-day 820 call

This creates a structure that profits if the underlying stock stays near $800, and also benefits from IV contraction post-earnings.

3. Adjustment-Friendly Framework

Unlike static spreads, diagonals **invite campaign-style layering and rolling.** Since one leg is long-term, it acts as an anchor around which the trade can evolve.

Adjustment Options Near Pivots:

- If price breaks above the pivot: roll the short strike higher for more credit
- If price stays range-bound: let the short leg expire and sell another
- If price pulls back: roll the short strike down or convert into a vertical

Example Campaign Trade:

- **Underlying:** A smartphone company's stock is trading at $170
- **Pivot zone:** $168–172
- **Strategy:** Buy 60-day 170 call, sell 15-day 172.5 call
- **Price stalls** at $172 → roll short leg to 175 for credit and extend campaign

This dynamic **trade evolution around the pivot** allows you to maintain exposure while reducing cost basis over time.

4. Campaign Trader's Takeaway

Diagonal spreads near pivot zones offer the **perfect mix of structure and flexibility:**

- You get **theta decay on the short leg**
- You keep **a directional anchor with the long leg**
- You position yourself for **low-risk income and high-reward roll potential**

By layering trades around pivot zones using diagonals, campaign traders can:

- Capitalize on IV skew and mean reversion
- Adjust quickly based on price behavior
- Build trades that are responsive to changing market conditions

Whether you're staging into a move, fading a breakout, or bracing for reversion, diagonals near pivot zones give you the **tools to stay adaptive, manage risk, and control your narrative.**

In the next section, we'll explore how **IV divergence and time-based decay** in double diagonals can enhance this approach even further—especially when the pivot zone becomes a volatility magnet.

C. Constructing and Managing IV-Divergent Positions

IV divergence occurs when the implied volatility of the short leg (usually near-term) is **significantly higher** than the long leg. This is common near earnings, Fed announcements, or geopolitical events.

To construct a **high-IV-divergent diagonal:**

- **Buy:** Longer-term option with stable IV (180–240 days out)
- **Sell:** Short-term option (30–45 days) with elevated IV due to event risk
- Choose **slightly OTM or ATM strikes** to align with the expected move

This structure benefits from:

- **IV contraction** after the event (short leg loses value quickly)
- **Theta decay** in the short leg
- **Vega protection** in the long leg (longer-term premium decays slower)

D. Adjusting Diagonals: Strike Distance, Expiration Mismatch, Skew

The true power of diagonals lies in their **adjustability:**

- **Strike Distance:** Widen or narrow the gap between long and short strikes depending on market momentum.
- **Expiration Mismatch:** Roll short legs forward or backward to capture premium or reduce risk.
- **Skew Adjustments:** Shift from call diagonals to put diagonals if volatility skew favors downside premium.

These micro-adjustments are part of the campaign mindset: building, adapting, and controlling trades as markets evolve around pivot zones.

Implied Volatility (IV) divergence is one of the most powerful market inefficiencies campaign traders can exploit. It occurs **when short-term options are priced with significantly higher IV than longer-term options**. This is especially common near **scheduled events** like earnings announcements, Fed decisions, CPI releases, or geopolitical developments.

By capturing the differential between inflated short-term IV and relatively stable longer-term IV, campaign traders can construct diagonals with a **built-in edge.**

Why It Works:

This structure benefits from multiple market dynamics:

- **IV Contraction:** After the event passes, short-term IV often drops sharply ("IV crush"), reducing the short leg's value
- **Theta Decay:** Time decay works in favor of the seller; short-term options lose value faster
- **Vega Protection:** The long leg's slower decay preserves position value and allows rolling/redeployment

Adjusting Diagonals: Strike Distance, Expiration Mismatch, Skew. The true strength of diagonals is not just in the initial setup—it's in the adjustability, which makes them ideal for campaign-style management.

1. Strike Distance Adjustments

- **Narrow Spread:** For slow, sideways markets where IV is likely to fall
- **Wider Spread:** For trending environments where directional bias is strong

Example:

- A smartphone stock stalls at a pivot zone

- Trader narrows the diagonal from 150/152.5 to 150/151 for tighter risk control

2. Expiration Mismatch (Rolling)

- Roll the **short leg forward** to the next weekly cycle to extend the time decay collection
- Roll **closer to the long leg's expiration** to transition into a vertical or unwind

Example:

- SPX trade: Buy 30-day 4200 call / Sell 5-day 4250 call
- Price stalls → roll short to next 5-day cycle to collect additional premium

3. Skew Adjustments: Calls vs. Puts

- If volatility skew favors puts (higher IV in OTM puts), shift to **put diagonals**
- Useful in **bearish markets** or when downside hedging is in demand

Example:

- An EV manufacturing stock shows downside skew pre-Fed
- Trader pivots from a call diagonal to a put diagonal (buying 230 put, selling 220 put short-term)

Campaign Trader Mindset: Build, Adapt, Control

Campaign traders treat diagonals as **strategic scaffolding:**

- Set up an initial position with IV edge and technical alignment
- Monitor price action and IV behavior around the pivot
- Roll, adjust, or scale based on evolving probabilities

This method transforms a single entry into a **multi-stage, adaptable campaign**, with control over risk, reward, and capital deployment.

Master Tip: Use platforms like TradeStation to monitor IV term structure and strike-level skew before selecting strikes and expirations.

In the next section, we'll explore how **double diagonals** allow even broader pivot coverage and multiple profit zones—ideal for volatile chop or wide consolidation ranges.

E. Using Pivot Zones for Campaign-Style Trade Layering

Rather than "all-in" trades, campaign traders **layer diagonals** around pivot zones:

- **Initial Entry:** Slightly bullish or bearish diagonal around the pivot
- **Additions:** If the market re-tests the pivot, add another diagonal closer to the money
- **Rolling Adjustments:** Shift the short strike as price moves away from the pivot
- **Exit Scaling:** Peel off short legs or full spreads as theta and gamma decay plays out

Layering trades near pivots reduces entry timing pressure and helps build asymmetric profiles that reward patience, discipline, and structure.

Conclusion

Trading pivots are more than just technical markers—they are the **strategic heartbeat** of campaign-style trading. These zones reflect market psychology, institutional memory, and high-volume transaction points that frequently serve as inflection areas. When campaign traders align their spreads with these pivot zones, they tap into a **predictive framework** that improves both timing and tactical precision.

The use of **diagonal and double diagonal spreads** around these pivots provides a rich blend of:

- **Theta harvesting:** Capitalizing on time decay, especially in high-IV short legs
- **IV reversion plays:** Selling elevated IV and benefiting from post-event normalization
- **Dynamic adjustment paths:** Flexibility to roll, expand, or shift positions based on real-time price interaction with pivots

Chapter: 5

Pivot Strategy Case Studies: Initial Set Up and Adjustments

A. Criteria for selecting the underlying stock: volatility, trend, and liquidity

At the heart of a successful Pivot strategy is smart stock selection. While most traders instinctively chase volatility, the Pivot is unique—we aren't looking for explosive daily movers. Instead, we're targeting stocks where historical volatility (HV) is contracting, and the price trend is becoming more orderly. These conditions allow us to exploit theta decay from the short legs while maintaining the strategic leverage of our long-dated straddle.

You might be thinking:

"Wait a minute, Tom—are you saying I should be looking for lower volatility stocks in a high-volatility market? That feels counterintuitive!"

It does at first—but with the right screening tools and market awareness, this becomes not only possible, but optimal. Here's how.

1. Volatility Trends: Focus on Contraction, Not Just Levels

Start by looking for stocks where HV has steadily declined over the past 4–8 weeks. These names often shift from chaotic to calm behavior—setting the stage for range-bound price action, which is perfect for adding the short legs of the Pivot.

Use ATR (Average True Range): A declining ATR suggests shrinking daily movement.

Check IV Rank/Percentile: A falling IV Rank (< 30%) means the market is no longer pricing in major moves.

Compare HV to IV: If HV is declining but IV remains elevated, you have a pricing edge—options are still rich, but movement is contained.

2. Trend Stability: Structure Over Surge

The ideal underlying stock for a Pivot is trending—but not ripping. You want a calm, predictable movement, typically in a channel or near technical consolidation zones.

Use Moving Averages: Stocks hugging the 20-day or 50-day SMA show structural strength.

MACD Flattening or Converging: Suggests momentum exhaustion—another good sign for theta harvesting.

Bollinger Band Narrowing: A sign of volatility compression, often preceding tight-range behavior.

3. Liquidity: The Hidden Engine of Execution

No strategy succeeds if you can't get in or out efficiently. Pivot trades involve multiple legs, often in monthly or weekly expirations—you need tight bid-ask spreads and decent open interest.

Minimum daily volume: 1M+ shares

Options open interest: >500 contracts per leg

Bid/Ask spreads: < $0.10 for the strikes you're trading

If you're dealing with thinly traded options, your campaign will suffer from slippage, poor fills, and execution delay—which directly erodes the fine margins a Pivot structure depends on.

4. Reality Check: What You're Probably Watching… Isn't the Best Candidate

Let's be honest—most traders build watchlists full of big names, momentum movers, and news-sensitive stocks. On big down days (like -1000-point drops in the Dow), those names all light up red. I've been there. I've had lists that look like a sea of red, too.

But those aren't your Pivot candidates.

Instead, you need to look outside your core list. Find secondary movers—stocks with lower beta, stable earnings visibility, or strong institutional support that tend to absorb market shocks better. These are often:

Sector laggards during index rallies

Non-headline tickers with predictable technical behavior

Stocks with quiet institutional accumulation near key levels

These names don't make the evening financial news—but they do set up beautifully for controlled campaigns with layered risk and time-based decay capture.

5. Be Intentional

Don't treat stock selection for Pivots like throwing darts at a momentum board. Be precise. Be patient. The right underlying stock is the foundation of your edge—get that right, and the rest of the trade structure will work with you, not against you.

In the next section, we'll explore how to determine when to overlay the short legs on your straddle and how to select the optimal strikes and expirations based on technical behavior.

6. What Happens after the Initial Entry: When the Fun Begins

Once the trader has selected the underlying stock and is positioned in a Straddle or Strangle, the trader then watches market movement and the selected stock's movement closely to determine the anticipated overall direction. Is the Volatility about to end and settle at a specific level or begin to trend in a direction?

We must watch our charts and analyze them just like we were Day Trading. But as I discussed in previous books, I typically start with a 15-minute chart and then analyze 5-minute and 1-minute chart before entering the next phase of the trade, which would be accompanying short legs to the already entered long call and put legs.

B. Finding Pivot stocks using Searches

Firebird offers 2 types of searches to find these stocks:

1. Manual Searches using the TradeStation Scanner and
2. Continuous Searches using the TradeStation RadarScreen

a. Searches using the TradeStation Scanner

The TradeStation Scanner is ideal for finding these stocks because it can be used to search all stocks to identify optionable stocks, that have decreasing volatility, relative strength and enough option open interest to point to tight enough spreads to trade. You can see these criteria shown in the TradeStation Scanner PopUp box shown below. You will also notice that an additional search criteria is being used to further select stocks that would improve the success of Pivot Trading, the Firebird Pivot Skew Search.

Scanner Pivot Search Set Up

TradeStation Technologies Inc. All Rights Reserved

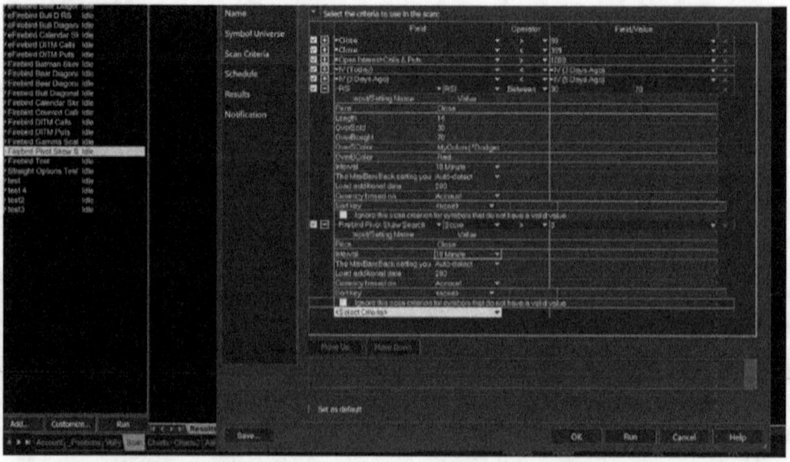

This scan runs very quickly and will show results in less than a minute or 2 max.

The results for this scan are shown below.

Results of this Scanner Pivot Search

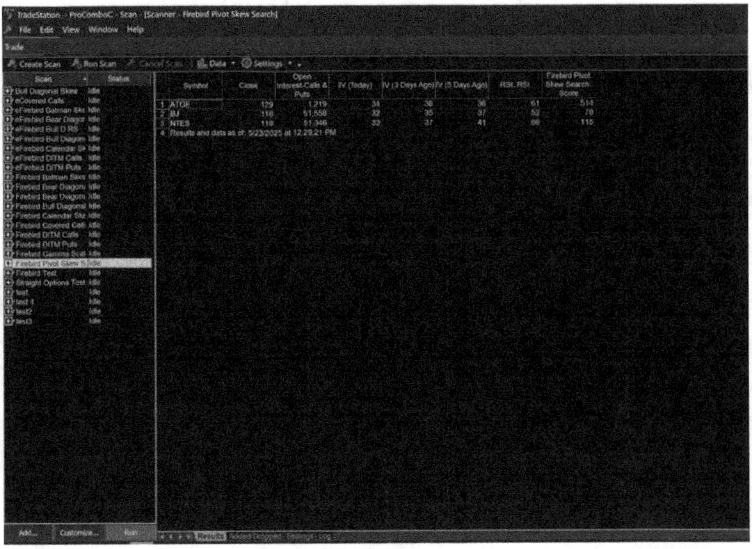

For this scan 3 possible underlying stocks are identified. The next step would be to analyze Straddles and Strangles in the TradeStation Option Station tool.

b. Searches using the TradeStation RadarScreen

A single TradeStation RadarScreen can be used to search about 2000 stocks continuously. I have set mine up in groups of stock prices, 89 to 125, 125 to 199, 200 to 299, and 300 to 399. I don't typically analyze and build option spread positions for stocks with prices over 399. The logic behind this is explained in my first book.

The search tool used for the Pivot searches, Firebird Pivot Skew Search, used for the RadarScreen, incorporates all of the criteria used in the Scanner search criteria and Firebird Scanner tool: optionable stocks, that have decreasing volatility, relative strength and enough option open interest to point to tight enough spreads to trade.

Below is a screenshot of the RadarScreen set up with several Firebird tools performing continuous searches, including the Firebird Pivot Skew Search.

RadarScreen Pivot Search Set Up

TradeStation Technologies Inc. All Rights Reserved

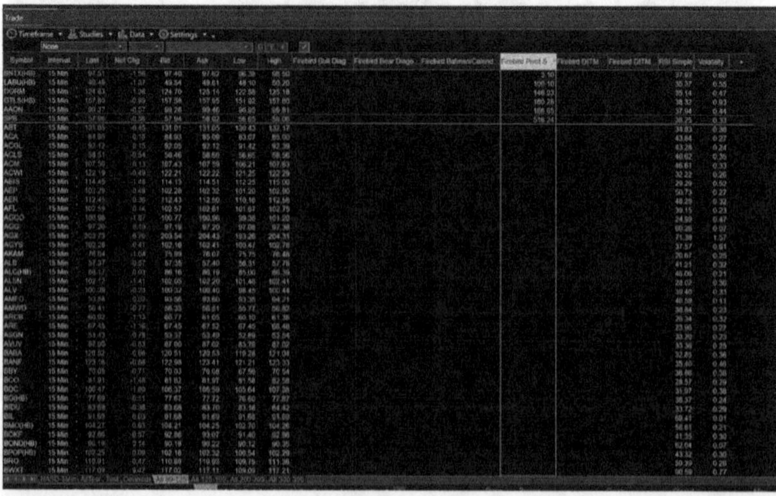

To get all of the stocks that are found in this RadarScreen to pop to the top as is shown in the Screenshot, just double click on the column heading. The higher Pivot scores should yield those with the best criteria for analysis in the TradeStation Option Station.

C. Entering the Straddle or Strangle

Establishing the core of your Pivot trade begins with careful construction of the initial long Straddle or Strangle. This foundational position sets the tone for the entire campaign, so it must be approached with strategy, precision, and alignment to your market outlook and volatility expectations.

1. Selecting the Strike Price for the Initial Straddle or Strangle

The success of a Straddle or Strangle begins with strike selection—and that's not as simple as just "getting close" to the stock price. You need to consider the expected movement range, support and resistance zones, and how much premium you're willing to pay upfront.

- **For a Straddle, the goal is to buy a Call and a Put at the same strike, usually ATM (At-the-Money).** This setup benefits from a sharp move in either direction, and the gamma sensitivity is maximized when the price stays close to the strike initially.

- **Best for:** Stocks near key breakout levels, upcoming events, or technical pivots.
- **Example:** XYZ trading at $100 — Buy $100 Call and $100 Put.

- For a Strangle, you widen the wings: Buy an OTM Call and an OTM Put, both slightly outside the current trading range.
  - **Best for:** Stocks with wider expected ranges or to reduce premium costs.
  - **Example:** XYZ at $100 — Buy $105 Call and $95 Put.

While the Straddle is more sensitive to immediate price movement, the Strangle offers cheaper entry, albeit with a lower delta at initiation. Choose based on:

- Expected price drift
- Volatility environment
- How quickly do you expect the trade to begin moving

You don't need to over-engineer the strike—you need to align it with the market story behind the chart.

2. Choosing Straddle or Strangle Expiration Dates

This is where many traders go wrong: they buy short-term options expecting long-term movement. In campaign trading, we build time into the trade to let the thesis unfold and to give ourselves room to adjust, overlay short legs, and harvest premium.

For Pivot campaigns, the long options should have an expiration of 4 to 6 months out. This timeframe accomplishes several goals:

- **Reduces theta decay impact**
- **Preserves delta stability for hedge decisions**
- **Allows repeated use of short-term short legs for income**

Longer-dated options offer a better balance of delta and gamma, while retaining value longer as the campaign evolves. They also withstand short-term price noise, making it easier to stay committed to the position through whipsaws.

Typical Expiration Guidelines:

- **5–6 months for initial long straddle/strangle**
- **Weekly or monthly options for short legs added later (discussed in Pivot overlays)**

A long-dated Straddle acts like flexible infrastructure—you're not rushing to be right. Instead, you're setting up a position that can adapt as the market develops.

Pro Tip: Match Volatility with Expiration

If you're entering a Straddle/Strangle when implied volatility is low but expected to rise, you may also benefit from vega exposure. A long-dated position will gain in value as IV rises.

But if IV is already elevated, you must manage premium risk carefully. In that case, favor a slightly shorter expiration or scale the position smaller and prepare to layer in short legs sooner.

Framework for a Campaign

The long Straddle or Strangle is not just a static bet—it's the flexible framework for a campaign. You're building a position that will eventually evolve with short overlays, rolls, or directional exits. But the first step must be solid: align strike and expiration with your forecast for volatility, price movement, and trade duration.

Up next: we'll examine how to overlay short legs onto this core position to create the full Pivot structure—and the decision logic behind whether to stay passive or go active with income layers.

D. Strategic Overlay – Short Leg Decisions in the Pivot Campaign

The Pivot strategy is an advanced campaign trade that begins with **a long-dated at-the-money (ATM) straddle or strangle**—a powerful, volatility-driven position that offers two-sided exposure. The unique aspect of the Pivot is the addition of short-dated, short option legs that create time-based overlays to harvest theta and shape profit zones. These short legs, typically placed 3–5 weeks out, are not mandatory—they are strategic. This chapter explores when and why to add them, how to select the optimal strikes, and what to do as expiration nears.

1. The Foundation: Long-Dated Straddle/Strangle

The campaign begins with establishing a 6-month ATM straddle (or a slightly OTM strangle, depending on cost and outlook).

Example:

XYZ stock is trading at $100. The trader opens:

- **Long 1x $100 Call (6 months out)**
- **Long 1x $100 Put (6 months out)**

This creates:

- A close to delta-neutral, vega-positive, gamma-neutral position.
- A large potential profit zone if the stock makes a significant move in either direction.
- Exposure to implied volatility (IV) increases, ideal for pre-event or macro uncertainty setups.

Why begin with a straddle?

- It's a **foundation trade** for volatility expansion.
- It requires no directional bias.
- It provides flexibility for future layers (e.g., the Pivot overlay).

2. When to Add the Short Legs to Create a Pivot

After initiating the long straddle, the trader monitors the **price behavior, volatility environment**, and **technical signals**. The decision to overlay short calls and puts (typically with ~30 days to expiration) depends on:

- **Stock stagnation or range-bound behavior** (theta harvesting opportunity)
- **Volatility contraction** (IV mean-reversion opportunity)
- **Support/resistance interaction** (pivot zone defense

strategy)

Key Trigger Points for Adding Short Legs:

- Price stays near the original straddle strike for 5–10 trading sessions.
- IV Rank drops below 30%, suggesting options are overpriced.
- Bollinger Band contraction or MACD flattening suggests reduced near-term momentum.

At this point, the trader can **add short calls and puts** at targeted strikes to create a Pivot—a time-defined, shaped risk/reward zone.

3. Selecting the Strike Prices for Short Legs

Short legs in the Pivot trade are **tactical instruments**. They allow you to:

- Generate **income** from time decay
- **Cap exposure** to whipsaw movements
- Create a **temporary directional skew** in your straddle/strangle

Decision Matrix for Strike Selection:

Outlook	Short Call Strike	Short Put Strike	Rationale
Neutral (range-bound)	Just OTM ($102–$103)	Just OTM ($97–$98)	Capture premium near max decay while allowing room for movement
Slightly Bullish	Above resistance ($105–$107)	ATM or slightly ITM ($99–$100)	Allow upside room, reduce risk below
Slightly Bearish	ATM or slightly ITM ($100–$99)	Below support ($95–$96)	Collect downside decay, hedge rally risk

High IV, no bias	ATM ($100)	ATM ($100)	Maximum decay rate; short-term theta harvest

Example:

- XYZ at $100, long 6-month straddle in place.
- IV Rank = 25%, RSI flat, stock hovering at VWAP.
- Trader sells:
  - **1x $105 Call (30DTE)**
  - **1x $95 Put (30DTE)**

This creates a short strangle overlay that decays rapidly while the long straddle remains in place.

4. Risk Analysis – Straddle Alone vs. Pivot Overlay

Position	Pros	Risks
Long Straddle Only	Large directional gain potential, flexible	Theta decay, IV crush, no income from stagnation
Pivot (Straddle + Short Legs)	Collects premium, flattens gamma, adjusts skew	Risk of price breaching short legs, assignment risk near expiration

Breach Scenarios:

- If price **moves beyond** a short leg, the campaign may face **temporary directional pressure.**
- If left unmanaged, a strong breakout can create losses on the short leg that **exceed the gains** in the long straddle—especially near expiration.
- Active traders can **roll, convert**, or **delta hedge** short legs based on movement.

5. Managing the Pivot Near Expiration

Short legs near expiration require close attention. As they decay, the gamma risk increases, particularly if the underlying is near a short strike.

Decision Alternatives:

1. Let Expire Worthless

- o If price remains safely between strikes and premium is minimal
- o Ideal for capturing full theta value

2. Close Early

- o If price approaches a short leg (within 1%–2%)
- o Protects against gamma explosion and assignment risk

3. Roll Forward

- o Extend campaign by selling next month's legs at adjusted strikes
- o Aligns with evolving market direction or event calendar

4. Convert to Diagonal or Vertical

- o For directional bias, roll the short leg ITM and reposition
- o Helps define risk and realize gains from original position

What to do Now? Possible Future Adjustments

With profit in hand from the expired short put, the trader will benefit if the underlying stock stays close to the same price or moves back up a bit. One possible way to manage this scenario is to hold until the next month when the short options are all decayed away and close the position. That is if the trader is so lucky and the stock does not make more big moves.

E. Initial Risk Assessment and Potential Rewards for Pivot Campaigns

The **Pivot strategy**—built on a long-dated Straddle or Strangle, overlaid with short-term option legs—offers campaign traders a highly flexible and powerful structure. It is especially effective in volatile markets where direction is uncertain, but price is expected to oscillate within a defined range. To trade this strategy effectively, it's critical to evaluate both the **initial risks and the potential for returns**, not just at entry but over the course of the trade's evolution.

1. Assessing Risk in a Pivot Structure

Risk in a Pivot campaign is multidimensional. It stems from the capital required to open the long Straddle/Strangle, the potential obligation of the short-term legs, the behavior of implied volatility, and the passage of time. Let's break this down:

❖ **Maximum Potential Loss**

- **Long Straddle/Strangle Core:** The cost of the long legs (calls and puts 5–6 months out) represents the maximum risk **before any short legs are sold**. This is a debit trade upfront, and the capital committed is significant. For example:
    - Buy 1 Jan $100 Call for $12
    - Buy 1 Jan $100 Put for $11
    - Total risk (initial debit) = **$2,300**
- **Adding the Pivot Legs (Short-term Calls and Puts):**
    - When short-term options are sold against the long legs (weekly or monthly), they **reduce the net cost but introduce assignment and directional risk** if the stock moves aggressively.
    - Traders must consider the **exposure from the short legs,** especially near expiration, where gamma risk increases.

Key Risk Principle: The long legs provide defined risk, but the short legs can increase short-term directional risk if price moves outside the expected range.

❖ **Time Decay (Theta Exposure)**

- **The Edge of the Pivot:** Time decay works in your favor when managing short legs that are sold repeatedly.
- The **long legs** decay slowly due to extended expiration, while

short legs decay rapidly, offering consistent income potential.

However, if the underlying stalls too long, theta can slowly erode the long position's value—especially if short premium sales are not sized or timed correctly.

❖ **Volatility Impact (Vega Sensitivity)**

- The long Straddle/Strangle benefits from an **increase in IV,** particularly after entry. But if IV contracts suddenly (post-news, post-Fed, post-earnings), the long options lose value quickly.
- Short legs are **most effective when IV is elevated**, allowing you to **sell rich premium**. But beware: if IV spikes **after** you sell short legs, the position can move against you faster.

TIP: Always check **IV Rank** and IV **percentile** before overlaying short legs.

2. Evaluating Potential Rewards

The Pivot shines when used as an **active income engine**. Its payoff comes from both volatility exposure and short premium harvesting:

❖ **Premium Decay Income**

- Selling short puts and calls at opportune levels (above/below resistance/support or IV peaks) allows you to collect premium **without fully risking directional exposure.**
- Over time, multiple short cycles can **offset a large portion of the initial debit** spent on the Straddle/Strangle.

❖ **Movement Bonus**

- If the stock makes **controlled swings around the pivot strike,** you can repeatedly scalp premium on both sides.
- Partial directional moves also benefit the long options. A gradual trend toward one wing allows for diagonal rolls or vertical conversions to extract even more value.

Example:

- Initial Debit: $2,300
- Weekly short legs collected over 4 weeks: $300–$400/week
- Total reduction in cost basis: up to $1,600 within one month = 70%+ cost recovery

3. Balancing Risk and Reward: The Campaign Mindset

The key to Pivot trading is **not just the initial structure**—it's your **willingness to evolve the trade**. As market conditions shift, so must your management.

Strategic Adjustments

- **Rolling short legs:** Adjust strike or expiration based on delta movement or IV shifts.
- **Converting long legs:** If price trends, roll long options into a vertical or diagonal structure to lock in gains and reduce exposure.
- **Managing short leg risk:** Set alerts near short strike levels to prevent assignment or exit early.

Conclusion: The Power of the Pivot Trade

The decision to add short legs to a long-dated straddle should be **strategic, not automatic**. The Pivot offers traders a way to shape and refine risk, collect **intermediate income,** and remain **flexible** as the campaign evolves. By aligning strike selection with technical levels and using IV context for timing, traders can extract value from time and volatility while managing risk with precision.

This structure embodies campaign-style thinking: **modular, adaptive, and resilient**—precisely what volatile markets demand.

Chapter: 6

Gamma Scalping Fundamentals – Strategy, Setup, and Selection

In a volatile market, few strategies offer the precision and adaptability of gamma scalping. While often overlooked by retail traders due to its active nature and complexity, gamma scalping is a cornerstone of campaign-style trading. It transforms volatility into an asset, capitalizing on price oscillations rather than forecasting market direction. Unlike directional plays that rely on price prediction or time-decay income strategies, gamma scalping thrives on the simple fact that markets move.

A. What Is Gamma Scalping and When Is It Used?

Gamma scalping is a delta-neutral trading technique that involves managing the changing delta of a long options position (typically at-the-money) by buying or selling shares of the underlying stock. As the stock moves and the delta shifts, the trader rebalances by adjusting their stock position, capturing profits in the process.

This strategy is typically used:

- In highly volatile markets where prices swing intraday
- When no strong directional bias exists
- Around major events like earnings or macroeconomic releases

Gamma scalping turns volatility into a tactical advantage rather than a risk to be hedged.

1. Core Concept of Gamma Scalping

The fundamental idea behind gamma scalping lies in understanding the interaction between **delta** and **gamma**:

- **Delta** represents how much the option price moves with a $1 change in the underlying.
- **Gamma** measures how much the delta changes as the underlying moves.

Since gamma is highest for **ATM options near expiration**, these positions are **very responsive to price movement**. Traders capitalize on this by:

1. **Buying low, selling high** as they rebalance the delta through stock trades.
2. **Locking in small profits** as the price whipsaws around a neutral level.

2. How It Works – Example Scenario

- **Stock XYZ is trading at $100.**
  - A trader buys 10 ATM calls with delta of 0.50 → Total delta = +500.
  - The trader sells 500 shares of XYZ to create a **delta-neutral** position.

If stock rises to $101:

- Delta of options increases to 0.60 → Total delta = +600.
- Trader sells another 100 shares of stock → Maintains delta-neutral position.

If stock drops back to $100:

- Option delta decreases to 0.50 → Total delta = +500.
- Trader **buys back** 100 shares → Locks in profit on the way down.

Over time, these buy-sell cycles result in net positive returns **even if the stock doesn't trend.**

3. Ideal Conditions for Gamma Scalping

Gamma scalping works best when:

- **Volatility is high and erratic:** Prices swing intraday, giving more opportunities to scalp.
- **No strong directional bias exists:** The trader benefits more from oscillation than trending moves.
- **Options are near-the-money and close to expiration:** Higher gamma means faster delta shifts. But hold options that

are further from expiration also works.

- **The trader can monitor the market actively:** Gamma scalping requires precise, often intraday adjustments.

B. Market Environments Where Gamma Scalping Excels

Gamma scalping is especially effective when:

- Implied volatility is high, causing option gamma to increase
- Intraday or short-term price movement is frequent and sharp
- The trader expects movement but not necessarily a sustained trend

Examples of ideal environments include:

- Federal Reserve announcement weeks
- Earnings season for high-beta stocks
- Market correction phases, where price oscillates wildly within a range

Important Considerations

- **Transaction Costs:** Frequent rebalancing can eat into profits if spreads and commissions are high.
- **Execution Speed:** Traders must act quickly to maintain delta-neutrality in fast-moving markets.

Discipline: Profitable gamma scalping requires strict adherence to rules—not emotional reaction.

Before we move to the next section, let's get a summary from ChatGPT about the best markets in which to use Gamma Scalping.

Prompt

Develop a 1 1/2-page document describing the best market characteristics for using Gamma Scalping and include the factors used to determine the characteristics of the market. Also provide an example of how to find a good stock to be used for Gamma Scalping.

Response with ChatGPT

Here is a 1½-page document describing the ideal market conditions for gamma scalping, along with the key indicators and a practical stock selection example:

Ideal Market Characteristics for Gamma Scalping

Gamma scalping is a high-precision, non-directional trading strategy designed to thrive in fast-moving and volatile markets. Unlike directional options strategies that profit from trending moves or income strategies that rely on time decay, gamma scalping profits from price fluctuations around a strike price—independent of the direction of those moves. To execute this strategy successfully, traders must identify market conditions that naturally favor frequent price reversals and elevated short-term volatility.

Key Market Characteristics for Gamma Scalping

1. High Realized Volatility with No Strong Directional Trend

Gamma scalping works best in markets where the underlying asset exhibits wide intraday swings, but without sustained one-way movement. A stock that oscillates within a defined price range over multiple sessions is ideal. Look for:

- *Daily trading ranges > 1.5% of the underlying stock price*
- *Multiple intraday reversals or range-bound action around a key strike*

2. Moderate to High Implied Volatility (IV)

A heightened implied volatility environment increases option premiums and amplifies gamma sensitivity. Gamma scalpers prefer IV, that is:

- *Elevated but not extreme (IV Rank between 40–70%)*
- *High enough to provide responsive delta changes in ATM options*
- *Stable enough to avoid sudden crashes (e.g., post-earnings)*

3. Tight Liquidity and Narrow Bid-Ask Spreads

Execution quality is critical. Gamma scalping requires frequent adjustments of the stock position to remain delta-neutral. Illiquid underlyings or wide bid/ask spreads can erode profits through slippage and transaction costs. The best candidates offer:

- *Option bid-ask spreads under $0.10 for ATM options*
- *Stock spreads ≤ $0.02*
- *Open interest ≥ 500 contracts for ATM options*

4. Availability of Weekly Options

Shorter expiration cycles increase gamma sensitivity and allow more responsive delta shifts. Stocks with active weekly expirations provide more granular control for scalping.

5. Technical Conditions Supporting Volatility

Chart setups such as wedge patterns, Bollinger Band expansions, or RSI divergences around pivot zones often signal prime environments for gamma scalping. Use:

- *ATR (Average True Range) > 2% of price*
- *Bollinger Band width expansion*
- *VWAP reversion setups*

How to Identify a Strong Gamma Scalping Candidate

Step-by-Step Example: Selecting a Stock

Stock Candidate: NVDA (NVIDIA Corporation)

NVDA is a highly liquid tech stock that frequently shows strong intraday movement without committing to long-term trends.

1. Check Liquidity and Volume

- *Average daily stock volume > 30M shares*
- *ATM options with > 1000 contracts open interest*
- *Bid/ask spreads on options < $0.05*

2. Analyze Volatility Metrics

- *Current IV = 50%*
- *IV Rank = 55% (mid-range → options are priced above average)*
- *Realized Volatility (20-day) = 48%*
- *IV and RV are closely aligned—suggesting tradable movement is occurring*

3. Evaluate Price Action

- *Trading range over last 5 days: $415–$440*
- *Intraday price swings of 1.5–2.0%*
- *RSI frequently diverging near Bollinger band edges*
- *Price consolidating near VWAP—a high-likelihood reversion zone*

4. Technical Setups

MACD and ADX signal low trend strength → confirms range-bound potential

- *Bollinger Bands widening → likely continuation of choppy volatility*

This setup provides the right ingredients: liquid options, price range with predictable reversals, and gamma-responsive short-term options. A gamma scalper could establish a delta-neutral position using 5–10 ATM calls or puts and hedge with stock on each $1 swing, collecting small profits from each round trip.

Conclusion

The ideal environment for gamma scalping is not simply a "volatile" market—it is a volatile, non-trending, and liquid one. Traders who learn to recognize this unique market signature, and apply structured stock screening tools, can use gamma scalping to turn volatility into a systematic edge. Selecting the right stock or index is just as important as the execution, and the best results come when strategy meets structure.

C. Practical Trading Level Description

Gamma scalping is a **discipline-heavy, volatility-focused trading approach** that seeks to exploit rapid delta changes by actively adjusting the underlying stock position. It is not about predicting where the stock will go, but **profiting from the fact that it moves.**

In the hands of a well-prepared campaign trader, gamma scalping becomes a tactical tool **for intraday and multi-day income generation,** particularly when uncertainty and volatility dominate the market environment.

Gamma scalping requires:

- A long options position (typically at-the-money)
- A real-time delta tracker or platform that supports options Greeks
- A willingness and ability to trade the underlying stock quickly and frequently

Traders must monitor their total net delta and execute corresponding stock trades to maintain neutrality. Execution tools and tight spreads are essential, making platforms like TradeStation or professional-grade dashboards highly preferred.

Example:

- o You own 10 ATM calls on SPX and short 500 shares to stay neutral.
- o As price rises and falls, you adjust your short position by buying/selling stock.
- o Each adjustment locks in small gains—buying low and selling high repeatedly.

2. No Reliance on Theta (Time Decay):

- o Time decay is a cost, not a benefit.
- o Gamma scalpers usually own long options, which lose value over time.
- o The goal is to offset theta decay with repeated profits from price movement.

3. Reactionary, Not Predictive:

- o Directional traders enter based on a thesis: "XYZ is going to $150."
- o Gamma scalpers say: "I don't care where it goes—I'll adjust as it moves."
- o This is a strategy based on engagement and flexibility, not forecasting.

Takeaway: Understanding the Gamma Scalping Process

This graphic illustrates the **core mechanics and philosophy** behind gamma scalping—an active options strategy designed to thrive in fast-moving, volatile market environments.

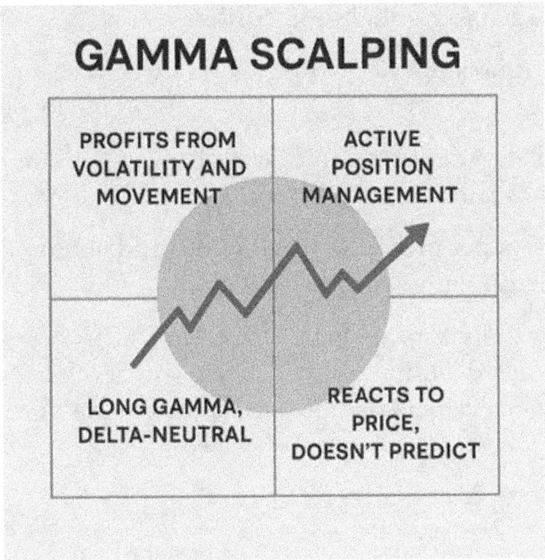

Dynamic Delta Adjustment

- As the price of the underlying asset moves, the **delta** of the long options position changes.
- Traders **rebalance** by buying or selling the underlying stock to maintain a **delta-neutral** exposure.
- These rebalancing trades are typically small, frequent, and precise—executed mechanically throughout the day or over multiple days.

Example:

- SPY is trading at $420, and a trader holds 10 ATM call options (delta ~0.50 each = +500 total delta).
- To neutralize delta, the trader sells 500 shares.
- If SPY rises to $422 and delta increases to 0.60 each (now +600 delta), the trader sells an additional 100 shares.

- If SPY falls back to $420, delta drops to 0.50 again, and the trader **buys back** 100 shares—**locking in a profit** from the volatility.

Gamma Enables Scalping Profits

- **Gamma** is the Greek that allows delta to change rapidly with price.
- Higher gamma = faster delta changes = more opportunities to rebalance.
- The scalper profits by **buying low and selling high** as prices whip around the central strike.

Analogy: Think of gamma as the engine of a car—delta is the speed. Gamma determines how quickly you accelerate or decelerate (delta change). Scalpers use this acceleration to shift gears at the right moment.

Controlled, Mechanical Process

- Gamma scalping is not an emotional or predictive game—it's about **precision, repetition, and neutrality.**
- There is no need to forecast direction. The trader adapts to what the market gives, using delta adjustments as a systematic tool to extract gains.

Key Tools for Execution:

- Live delta tracking via a trading platform like TradeStation
- Alerts for delta drift or price thresholds
- Transaction logs and journaling for review and optimization

D. Gamma Scalping – A Completely Different Mindset

Gamma scalping challenges conventional trading psychology. It demands a shift away from prediction and toward mechanical responsiveness.

1. Position-Neutral by Design:

Gamma scalpers start delta-neutral. They are neither long nor short the market in directional terms, but instead position themselves to benefit from movement itself.

2. Profits from Movement, Not Direction:

Every time the stock moves, delta changes. Each adjustment—buying low, selling high—captures a small profit. Repeating this across intraday swings builds a scalable edge.

3. No Reliance on Theta (Time Decay):

Unlike income strategies, gamma scalping doesn't rely on time passing. In fact, time decay (theta) is a headwind. Traders mitigate this by using short-dated but not ultra-short options, maximizing gamma while managing theta.

4. Reactionary, Not Predictive:

Gamma scalpers respond to market movement. They do not predict or forecast price action. This mechanical nature requires discipline and a strong routine.

5. Key Traits for Gamma Scalping Mastery:

Constant Awareness

Gamma scalpers must maintain high situational awareness:

- Price can move quickly, altering delta exposure in seconds.
- Traders need to **monitor real-time data feeds, option Greeks, and stock behavior**—especially during news events or key technical levels.

Example: During an FOMC press conference, SPX may jump 30 points in 15 minutes. The scalper must adjust delta multiple times to stay neutral and extract gains.

Fast Execution

Speed is a performance edge. Gamma scalping requires:

- **Quick decision-making:** Hesitation can turn opportunity into loss.

- **Efficient order routing:** Use hotkeys, preset orders, and DMA platforms when possible.

Example: You notice your delta has moved to +400 after a sudden rally. Delaying a hedge could expose the trade to directional risk and miss the scalp.

No Ego Trading

Gamma scalping isn't about being "right" on market direction.

- This is a **reactionary strategy**, where profits come from volatility—not predictions.
- Great scalpers stay neutral and detached from outcome.

Mantra: "I'm not trying to beat the market—I'm harvesting the chop."

Journaling and Review

Consistent review builds skill.

- Log every adjustment: time, price, delta before/after, market conditions.
- Analyze the day's activity to spot overtrading, slippage, or missed opportunities.

Example Journal Entry:

- 10:05 AM: Sold 100 shares at $342.65 to reduce delta from +280 to +180 after SPY rallied.
- 10:45 AM: Bought 100 shares at $341.80 to rebalance delta after drop—locked in $85 scalp.

Transaction Cost Control

Frequent trades mean small inefficiencies can kill profitability:

- Use brokers with low commissions and tight bid/ask spreads.
- Avoid thinly traded stocks or options with wide spreads.

Example: A trader pays $0.65 per round-trip option trade and $0.01/share on stock. Over 20 adjustments, these costs could eat $100–200 of profits.

Essential Mindset and Discipline for Scalpers

Gamma scalping is as much a **mental discipline** as it is a technical strategy. While understanding delta and gamma is critical, lasting success comes from mastering the **psychological and procedural aspects** of this fast-paced approach.

Gamma scalping seems simple on paper: "Stay delta-neutral, scalp the swings." But in real time, the trader is navigating:

- Market noise
- Rapid delta shifts
- Execution delays
- Emotional fatigue

To succeed, traders must become **mechanical in behavior and objective in evaluation.**

- No chasing. No freezing. No revenge trades.
- Trust the edge, execute the plan.

Mindset Example:

- After three small winning scalps, a trader is tempted to over-size the next adjustment.
- A disciplined scalper resists this impulse, knowing that consistency—not jackpot thinking—builds the account.

Gamma scalping rewards the trader who is **present, precise, and psychologically prepared**. It's a craft of repetition and refinement.

Success isn't about one perfect trade—it's about **100 good adjustments** made with discipline, clarity, and a deep respect for market movement.

Mindset Takeaway

Gamma scalping is a **high-engagement strategy for advanced traders** who prefer to react to price instead of predict it. It thrives in **volatile markets,** rewards active risk management, and requires an adaptive mindset.

If directional and income strategies are like sailing with or against the wind, gamma scalping is like adjusting the sails constantly to capture the shifting breeze—**navigating not by destination, but by momentum.**

E. Why It's Not for Beginners

Gamma scalping is not suitable for novice traders. It involves:

- Rapid-fire execution of multiple trades
- Real-time monitoring of Greeks and market behavior
- Transaction cost sensitivity (slippage, commissions)

Beginners may find the active nature stressful or misinterpret delta/gamma relationships. Gamma scalping is best suited for intermediate-to-advanced traders with strong platform fluency and execution discipline.

- Gamma scalping requires constant monitoring of delta, pricing, and execution.
- Traders must be confident in calculating adjustments, reading volatility conditions, and handling rapid-fire decision-making.
- It demands **emotional neutrality**—reacting to movement without bias, and adjusting without hesitation.

Analogy: If most trading is like chess—planning three moves ahead—gamma scalping is like fencing: fast, reactive, precise.

Energy In, Energy Out

Volatility is often viewed as dangerous or uncertain—but to the prepared trader, it's the **fuel for profitability.**

- Gamma scalping allows you to **channel market energy** into consistent, mechanical profits.
- It's one of the few strategies where more volatility often **equals more opportunity.**

Example:

- A stock that oscillates ±2% intraday may present 3–4 rebalancing opportunities per day.

Over time, these scalps compound—creating consistent returns from controlled engagement.

F. Benefits of Gamma Scalping in a High-Volatility Regime

In high-volatility conditions, gamma scalping shines:

- Frequent Price Swings: Creates numerous adjustment opportunities
- Rich Option Premiums: Enhance gamma and responsiveness
- Delta Variability: Accelerates the movement of the hedge ratio
- Non-Directional Profits: Ideal when trends are unclear or fading

This strategy allows traders to "scalp the whips" of market energy without needing to guess the next major move.

Gamma scalping is one of the few strategies that **thrives in chaos.** When most traders fear volatility spikes, gamma scalpers see **an invitation to extract consistent gains**—not from predicting the future, but from staying engaged with real-time price action.

High-volatility regimes provide the perfect environment because:

- **Price moves frequently and sharply,** creating multiple intraday or intraweek opportunities to buy low and sell high.
- **Option premiums expand,** especially for near-the-money (ATM) options, increasing gamma and making delta shifts more sensitive and exploitable.
- **Reversals are common,** meaning price doesn't trend in one direction for long, and whipsaws provide fertile ground for harvesting gains through rebalancing.

Key Benefits of Gamma Scalping in Volatile Conditions

1. Non-Directional Profit Potential

Gamma scalping does not require the market to trend—it benefits from **movement in either direction.**

- The strategy is ideal during periods of news uncertainty, earnings seasons, or macroeconomic event risk.

2. Built-In Risk Control Through Adjustments

By constantly adjusting the delta back to neutral, gamma scalping **minimizes exposure to large directional moves**. This proactive management allows traders to control risk in real time.

- Unlike a static trade, the scalper is **always adjusting** to the market's tone.

Example:

- If an EV Manufacturing stock jumps $10 unexpectedly, the scalper sells shares to neutralize new delta exposure, locking in a profit on the long options.

3. Scalable with Capital and Experience

As traders gain experience with gamma dynamics, they can:

- Scale the number of options held (e.g., 5 contracts vs. 50)
- Use automation or trading bots for delta adjustments
- Allocate more capital toward stocks that behave well in volatile regimes

This allows seasoned traders to increase returns while maintaining structure and discipline.

4. Volatility Is the Opportunity

Most strategies suffer in high-volatility markets:

- Directional plays become whipsawed
- Premium-selling strategies suffer drawdowns from sudden moves

Gamma scalping, on the other hand, **becomes more effective** as volatility increases:

- More gamma = more frequent delta shifts = more chances to scalp
- Sudden reversals = more spread between high and low fill prices

Example:

- During a CPI announcement, QQQ whipsaws ±2% in minutes.
- Gamma scalpers positioned before the release can execute multiple adjustments within a short window—locking in profits while others are stuck in losing trades.

Thriving in Chaos

In high-volatility environments, most traders focus on **surviving the storm**. Gamma scalpers, however, are built to **thrive in turbulence.** With real-time adjustments, neutral exposure, and strategy flexibility, they turn wild price action into a series of small, controlled, and repeatable wins.

Gamma scalping transforms volatility from a source of fear into a **mechanism for consistent opportunity**—rewarding discipline, responsiveness, and deep understanding of delta-gamma interactions.

Summary Principles

- Stay **delta-neutral** to remove directional risk.
- Use **gamma sensitivity** to your advantage.
- Let **volatility work for you**, not against you.
- Maintain discipline, track performance, and execute with intention.

G. Selecting the Right Stocks and Options for Gamma Scalping

In this section, we'll take this concept from theory to application. You will learn:

- How to **select the right stocks and options** to support your scalping framework.
- How to **build and adjust positions** in a step-by-step, real-world context.
- How to apply **risk management techniques** that prevent slippage and protect capital.

By mastering these elements, you'll add one of the most sophisticated volatility tools to your trading arsenal.

Get ready to take your campaign trading to the next level—where strategy becomes structure, movement becomes opportunity, and volatility becomes your greatest ally.

The ideal candidates have:

- **High Liquidity:** Tight spreads in both stock and options
- **Regular Movement:** Intraday price swings of 1% or more
- **High Gamma Sensitivity:** At-the-money options with 6–8 months to expiration
- **IV Rank > 50%:** Indicates option premiums are elevated

Gamma scalping is a powerful, precision-driven strategy—but its success hinges on selecting the right instruments. Not every stock or option chain is suitable. To identify ideal candidates a process focusing on liquidity, volatility, gamma sensitivity, and structural efficiency in the options market is applied.

Key Criteria for Stock Selection: Liquidity, Volatility, and Range

When building a gamma scalping campaign, stock selection is as important as strategy. You need underlying instruments that move efficiently, respond dynamically to volatility, and allow for precise execution. The ideal gamma scalping candidate exhibits three core characteristics: **liquidity, volatility, and range.**

1. Liquidity: Seamless Execution is Non-Negotiable

- Gamma scalping requires frequent buying and selling of the underlying stock—sometimes multiple times within an hour.
- To prevent slippage, widen spreads, or failed executions, you must trade highly liquid stocks.

What to Look For:

- **Average Daily Volume** > 1 million shares
- **Tight Bid/Ask Spreads:** Ideally between $0.01–$0.03
- **Level II Depth:** A deep order book with minimal gaps

between price levels

Avoid:

- Illiquid small caps, penny stocks, or exotic tickers with wide spreads
- These increase the risk of slippage and make delta hedging unreliable

2. Volatility: Fuel for the Strategy

- Gamma scalping profits from movement—so the stock must move.
- A low-volatility ticker may leave the trader making unnecessary adjustments with little payoff.

What to Look For:

- **Historical Volatility** (HV) over 30% annualized
- **High Beta:** Stocks that amplify market moves
- **Catalysts:** Earnings, economic events, product launches, or sector rotation

Volatility Tools to Use:

- ATR (Average True Range): Measures daily volatility in dollar terms
- Implied Volatility Rank (IVR): Helps gauge current IV relative to history

3. Range: Intraday Opportunity Windows

- Stocks that move **1–3% intraday** and return to technical levels are ideal for repetitive scalping.
- Gamma scalpers thrive in environments where price **oscillates around a pivot** or mean-reverting area.

What to Look For:

- **Daily trading range** with multiple inflection points
- **Bollinger Band Width:** Wide bands suggest more price travel potential

- **Volume profile zones** where price frequently revisits

Top Categories of Stocks for Gamma Scalping

Tech Growth Names

- High volume, high volatility, event-driven

Leveraged ETFs

- 2x or 3x beta provides amplified price movement and intraday range

Volatility Products

- Respond directly to market fear and movement

Caution: While leveraged ETFs and volatility products move aggressively, they may have wider spreads and can require extra attention to cost and slippage.

Great gamma scalping starts with **selecting the right battleground.** Liquid, volatile, range-bound stocks allow for:

- Clean delta adjustments
- Predictable gamma exposure
- Consistent opportunity to profit from whipsaw moves

By aligning stock selection with your gamma strategy, you give yourself the mechanical efficiency and movement edge needed to turn volatility into repeatable profits.

4. Option Selection: Gamma, Strike Price Positioning, and Expiry Windows

After identifying the right stock, the success of your gamma scalping campaign depends on **selecting the right option contracts.** The goal is to maximize gamma sensitivity while keeping **theta decay and execution cost** under control. Choosing the correct strike price and expiration date is essential for optimizing how your delta reacts to price changes in the underlying asset.

Gamma Sensitivity: The Engine of Scalping

Gamma is the Greek that measures how fast delta changes. Since gamma scalping depends on **delta fluctuations**, you must target options that offer **the steepest gamma curve.**

Best Practice:

- Use **At-the-Money (ATM)** options for the highest gamma.
- Look for expirations with **6 to 8 months** remaining. This range:
  - Has adequate gamma sensitivity
  - Minimizes extreme theta decay experienced by ultra-short-term contracts

Avoid:

- Far OTM options—they have low gamma and won't adjust delta significantly
- Deep ITM options—they have stable delta and low gamma, reducing the opportunity to scalp

Strike Price Positioning

The positioning of your strike price defines your gamma exposure and potential responsiveness.

Best Choice:

- **ATM Strikes:** Ideal for pure gamma play
- **Slightly ITM Strikes:**
  - Use if you expect a directional bias
  - ITM strikes retain value better and reduce theta exposure, but sacrifice some gamma

Summary: What Makes a Great Gamma Scalping Option

- **ATM strike** for max delta change
- **6–8 Months to Expiration** for gamma edge with manageable theta
- **High open interest and tight spreads** for seamless execution
- **Slight ITM/OTM flexibility** to reflect your trade bias and scalp range

Remember: Your gamma scalping vehicle should respond to each dollar of movement like a finely tuned instrument—allowing you to act quickly and consistently, turning volatility into opportunity.

H. Using Scanners and Screeners to Identify Setups

Gamma scalping setups can be found using:

- Volatility Filters: IV Rank, IV Percentile, and Realized Volatility
- Liquidity Filters: Minimum 1M shares daily volume, option OI > 1,000

Custom screeners in platforms like TradeStation or Python scripts can alert to:

- ATM options with gamma > 0.08
- Stocks with ATR > 2% of price
- Narrow bid/ask spreads and dense option chains

Gamma scalping is a sophisticated, dynamic strategy that rewards preparation, speed, and discipline. By focusing on responsiveness over prediction and selecting the right setups, campaign traders can turn volatility into a reliable profit engine. In the next chapter, we'll explore how to execute and manage these positions in real time.

Using Scanners and Screeners to Identify Setups

Finding high-quality gamma scalping opportunities requires **a disciplined approach to screening**. With the right tools and filters, traders can isolate setups that offer the liquidity, volatility, and gamma profile needed for effective execution. This is where automation, intelligent scanning, and experience come together.

Liquidity Filters: Ensure Efficient Execution

To scalp effectively, your trading vehicle must offer **tight spreads and ample volume.** Gamma scalping involves frequent adjustments—so every penny of slippage matters.

Key Filters:

- **Stock Volume > 1M shares/day:** This ensures strong intraday movement and sufficient order flow.
- **Option Open Interest > 1,000** contracts (ATM strikes): Guarantees smoother fills and tighter bid/ask pricing.
- **Bid/Ask Spread < $0.10:** A tight spread reduces execution cost and improves trade efficiency.

Gamma Sensitivity Filters: Targeting High-Responsiveness Options

The **edge in gamma scalping lies in how fast delta shifts**. Use analytics platforms to pinpoint ATM options with steep gamma slopes.

Key Filters:

- **ATM Gamma** ≥ 0.05 per $1 move
- **Deltas between 0.45–0.55:** Ensures you're trading high gamma areas
- **Combine with Delta-Neutral Position Tools:** If possible, simulate positions and see how gamma shifts in real time

Trader's Edge Comes from Discipline + Screening

The best gamma scalpers don't chase—they **prepare**. They build custom scanners, refine filters, and focus only on names that meet their conditions.

Pro Tip: Journal every scan result and trade execution. Over time, patterns emerge that help refine your entries and avoid traps like:

- Low gamma
- Excessive theta burn
- High slippage from illiquidity

Final Thoughts

Gamma scalping **is not guesswork**—it's engineered. The strategy rewards:

- Consistent scanning
- Clear rules
- Fast reflexes
- High execution standards

By learning to **see volatility as an asset**, and not a threat, you transform uncertainty into your greatest advantage.

Chapter: 7

Executing and Managing the Dynamic Gamma Scalping Position

Gamma scalping is not a set-it-and-forget-it technique. It is a tactical, hands-on method that relies on mechanical execution, constant monitoring, and strategic rebalancing. In this chapter, we'll explore the complete lifecycle of a gamma scalping campaign: how to manage the position in real time, and optimize execution using market movement and volatility.

Building a Delta-Neutral Position with Calls or Puts

The foundation of a successful gamma scalping strategy is a **delta-neutral position** that allows the trader to profit from price oscillations rather than directional bias. This setup involves combining **long options** (calls or puts) with **offsetting positions** in the underlying stock to flatten directional exposure while retaining gamma sensitivity.

Why Delta-Neutral is Powerful in Gamma Scalping

Being delta-neutral doesn't mean you're static. It means your starting point is balanced, and every movement in price shifts delta due to gamma. **This creates rebalancing opportunities.**

As Price Moves:

- If an EV Manufacturer's stock rises to $905, the delta of the calls might increase to 0.60 → your position becomes **+300 deltas**
- To stay delta-neutral, **sell 50 additional shares** of stock
- If the stock later drops to $900 → delta falls to 0.50 → your position is **+250 deltas,** but now you're short 300 shares → **buy back 50 shares** to rebalance

Each time you buy low and sell high (or vice versa), **you harvest profit** without needing to predict the direction.

Key Reminders:

- Use **real-time delta calculations** to stay precise
- Monitor for **IV shifts**, as they affect gamma responsiveness
- Focus on **short-term ATM options** for the sharpest gamma

A delta-neutral setup is **not a passive position**—it's a starting point for dynamic management. By balancing long options with offsetting stock, the trader gains flexibility, control, and the ability to turn volatility into a revenue stream through frequent micro-adjustments.

Rebalancing Shares: How, When, and How Often

Once your delta-neutral gamma scalping position is established, the work is just beginning. The key to success lies in the **ongoing adjustments**—known as rebalancing. As the price of the underlying stock moves, the delta of your option position changes due to gamma. Your goal is to stay as close to delta-neutral as possible to maximize profits from these fluctuations.

How Rebalancing Works

Your options gain or lose delta as the underlying price moves. Each time delta shifts, your hedge (stock position) must shift too.

Step-by-Step Example:

- **Initial Position:** 5 ATM calls, delta = +0.50 each → +250 delta total
- You sell short 250 shares of stock to hedge → Net delta = 0
- Scenario A – Price Rises:
- XYZ rises from $900 to $902
- Delta increases from 0.50 to 0.60 per contract → +300 delta total
- To rebalance: Sell 50 additional shares to return to delta-neutral

Scenario B – Price Drops:

- XYZ drops from $902 to $899

- Delta drops from 0.60 to 0.40 → Total delta now = +200
- You're now short 300 shares → To rebalance, **buy back 100 shares (**300 − 200)

Each cycle of movement and rebalance creates small scalps: **sell higher, buy lower**, or vice versa—turning volatility into realized gains.

Guidelines for Rebalancing

Delta Shift Thresholds

Avoid reacting to every minor tick. Define a **delta range tolerance:**

- Rebalance when net delta deviates by ±**30 to 50 deltas**
- This gives room for movement without overtrading

Volatility-Based Frequency

- High Volatility (e.g., earnings weeks, macro events): Rebalance multiple times per hour if needed
- Low Volatility: Adjust every few hours or just 2–3 times a day

Example: If SPY is range-trading with 0.5% intraday volatility, you may rebalance once every 1–2 hours. If a stock is moving 3% per hour post-news, you may rebalance every 10–15 minutes.

Avoid Overtrading

Each adjustment involves:

- Transaction fees
- Bid/ask spread exposure
- Slippage

Too many small rebalances can erode profit. Make sure the expected gain from the adjustment outweighs the cost of executing it.

Rule of Thumb: If the price hasn't moved more than 1x your average spread + fee cost, it may not be worth adjusting.

Tools to Help

- Use **live delta readings** from your broker platform
- Create alerts for **net delta drift** using automation or scripts
- Track adjustments in a journal or spreadsheet to analyze frequency and impact

Rebalancing is where gamma scalping **comes alive**. It's how you turn the market's back-and-forth into a revenue stream. But it's also a discipline:

- Rebalance smartly
- Time your moves
- Weigh cost vs. benefit

Precision, patience, and preparedness turn a neutral position into a profit engine.

In the next section, we'll explore exactly how to **track delta shifts, set alerts, and execute stock trades** in rhythm with market action.

Tracking Delta Shifts, Buying/Selling Stock to Maintain Neutrality

At the heart of gamma scalping lies a simple—but powerful—concept: **delta neutrality is not static**. It fluctuates with every tick of the underlying stock, and the trader's edge comes from **constantly adjusting** to those shifts.

Professional gamma scalpers rely on robust platforms that provide **real-time delta readings**, but even independent traders can build reliable systems using spreadsheets, scripts, or broker tools.

Why Delta Shifts Matter

Delta measures **directional exposure**. In a gamma scalping setup, your long options gain or lose delta as the underlying stock moves. This changes your net position's risk profile—requiring you to buy or sell the stock to flatten exposure again.

The reverse is also true: if the price drops, your delta falls, and you must **buy shares** to offset the imbalance.

What to Monitor

To scalp effectively, monitor the following metrics:

- **Total Net Delta:** Combine delta from options and stock
- **Gamma per $1 Move:** Know how quickly delta will change with movement
- **Price Proximity to Strike:** ATM options have the highest gamma; once price moves away, gamma declines, and rebalancing slows

Executing Adjustments

Once a delta threshold is breached (e.g., ±30 deltas), execute a **market or limit order** to buy/sell stock.

Execution Tips:

- Use **limit orders** during low liquidity times to avoid slippage
- Trade **round lots (100 shares)** for optimal fills
- Use **bracket orders** or conditional orders to automate execution

You are essentially "scalping the whips"—buying low and selling high as price fluctuates around your core strike.

Each adjustment is a small gain captured through precision, speed, and discipline.

Tracking delta is not optional—it's **mission critical** in gamma scalping. The more accurate your readings and the faster your execution, the more reliable your edge.

Using Volatility to Your Advantage: "Scalp the Whips"

Gamma scalping thrives in fast-moving markets where prices **oscillate sharply** around a key strike price. Unlike directional strategies that require picking the "right" move, gamma scalping profits by **capitalizing on movement itself**—regardless of direction.

When Volatility Helps—and When It Doesn't

Gamma scalping works **best** in markets that are:

- **Choppy:** Prices oscillate around a mean or support/resistance level
- **Reactive:** Strong reversals after moves
- **Range-bound:** Lacking strong trending behavior
- **Avoid conditions like:**
- **Flat/stagnant ranges:** Without movement, theta decay eats away at the long option
- **Explosive trends without pullbacks:** May blow through your gamma before you can rebalance

Volatility Tips & Tactics

Use Technical Levels for Anticipation

Gamma scalping improves when you know where **price may reverse**. Key tools include:

- **VWAP (Volume Weighted Average Price):** Mean-reversion magnet during intraday action
- **Pivot Points:** Zones where traders expect a bounce or rejection
- **Bollinger Bands + RSI:** Help identify overextended moves likely to snap back

Pre-Plan Your Size

- Start with **smaller gamma** (e.g., 2–3 contracts)
- Add size as confidence grows or volatility conditions improve
- Avoid overexposing to illiquid stocks or wide bid/ask spreads

Set Alerts for Movement Triggers

- Price % movement (e.g., ±0.75%)
- Delta threshold breaches
- Gamma decay (if nearing expiration)

Key Takeaway:

Gamma scalping isn't about **prediction**—it's about precision.

When you recognize movement, lean into it. You're harvesting opportunity from volatility itself.

With each whip of the market, you respond—not react—with a small adjustment. Done consistently, those adjustments stack into **reliable, risk-controlled profits.**

Next, we'll bring it all together in a **real-world trade example,** tracking every hedge, scalp, and outcome step-by-step.

Conclusion

Executing a gamma scalping campaign is not a one-time setup—it's an **ongoing discipline**. This strategy demands **full engagement,** both mentally and technically. While many traders chase predictions, gamma scalpers **respond to reality**, turning unpredictable market motion into a structured, repeatable process for capturing gains.

What makes gamma scalping powerful is the **consistency of edge:**

- You don't need to guess direction
- You're not reliant on breakouts or trend continuation
- You're monetizing the market's natural rhythm—its indecision, overreaction, and reversion

All of this is achieved **without a strong directional opinion**—just responsiveness and execution precision.

Final Thoughts Before the Case Studies

To succeed with gamma scalping:

- **Commit to the mechanics:** Set delta thresholds, track gamma, and rebalance with purpose
- **Control transaction costs:** Use liquid instruments, minimize slippage
- **Log every move:** Build feedback into your strategy with journaling
- **Stay mentally composed:** Avoid revenge trades or overreacting to single swings

Chapter: 8

Gamma Scalping in Practice: A Real-World Example

Theory becomes power when applied. In this chapter, we walk through a detailed, real-world gamma scalping example to show how the concepts introduced earlier play out in live market conditions.

A. Case Study

This case study shows how a trader can execute a **gamma scalping strategy**—starting with the trade setup, managing delta changes, and locking in profits without betting on a directional move.

Trade Setup – XYZ Stock at $100

Scenario Overview:

- **Stock:** XYZ Corporation (highly liquid, tech sector)
- **Current Price:** $100.00
- **IV Rank:** 50% — meaning options are moderately expensive compared to the past year
- **Market Behavior:** No earnings or news, but XYZ moves up/down 1–2% daily
- **Range:** The stock has recently traded between $98 and $102

Trader's Goal:

Profit from the stock's back-and-forth movement—not from guessing direction—by staying delta-neutral and adjusting positions as the price shifts.

Step 1: Buy ATM Put Options

Details:

- **Position:** Buy 50 at-the-money (ATM) put options with 6 months to expiration
- **Strike Price:** $100
- **Delta (per option):** ~–0.40

- Gamma (per option): ~0.05
- Premium (per option): \$3.00
- Total Cost: 50 × 100 × \$3.00 = \$15,000

Step 2: Hedge the Delta

Each put has a delta of –0.40, meaning it gains \$0.40 for every \$1 drop in the stock.

- Total Delta from Puts:

  50 options × –0.40 delta × 100 shares = **–2,000 deltas**

  To balance this, the trader **buys 2,000 shares** of XYZ stock.

  - **Stock Position:** +2,000 shares
  - **Net Delta:** –2,000 (puts) + 2,000 (stock) = 0 deltas

The position is now delta-neutral but gamma-positive—ideal for scalping profits from movement.

Step 3: React to Price Movement

Gamma makes delta shift as the stock price changes. The trader adjusts the stock position to stay neutral.

If Price Rises to \$101

- Delta becomes less negative: approx. –0.35 per option
- New Total Delta = 50 × –0.35 × 100 = –1,750
- Trader initially owns 2,000 shares, so they **sell 250 shares** to stay neutral
- **Profit:** \$1 gain on 250 shares = **\$250**

If Price Drops to \$99

- Delta becomes more negative: approx. –0.45 per option
- New Total Delta = 50 × –0.45 × 100 = –2,250
- Trader owns initially 2,000 shares, so they **buy 250 shares** to rebalance
- **Profit:** \$1 gain on 250 shares = **\$250**

Key Takeaway

The trader isn't predicting where XYZ will go—they're reacting to movement and **locking in small profits** with each price swing. With enough volatility and active management, these scalps can add up to meaningful returns over time.

Why This Scenario Works

- **High IV Rank:** Options are expensive, gamma is high
- **No Events:** Price isn't anchored to news, encouraging oscillation
- **Defined Range:** Recent price action confirms a predictable, mean-reverting range

This forms an ideal backdrop for gamma scalping: **movement without momentum.**

B. Delta Calculations and Share Adjustments as Price Moves

Here's a step-by-step explanation of the gamma scalping example based on your scenario with delta-neutral adjustments and the stock returning to $100:

Initial Setup:

- **Options Purchased:** 50 ATM Puts (6-month expiry, strike = $100)
- **Delta per contract:** ~ -0.40 → Total Delta = -0.40 × 50 × 100 = -2000
- **Hedge:** Buy 2000 shares of XYZ at $100 to become delta-neutral

Price Movement and Adjustments:

1. Price moves to $101

- New Delta ≈ -0.35 × 50 × 100 = **-1750**
- Hedge: Sell **250 shares** (2000 - 1750) at $101
- Profit: $101 - $100 = $1 × 250 = **$250**

2. Price drops to $99

- New Delta ≈ -0.45 × 50 × 100 = -2250
- Hedge: Buy 500 shares (1750 → 2250) at $99
- Profit: Sold at $101, Bought at $99 = $2 × 250 = **$500**

3. Price rises to $100.5

- New Delta ≈ -0.375 × 50 × 100 = -1875
- Hedge: Sell 375 shares (2250 → 1875) at $100.5
- Profit: Bought at $99, Sold at $100.5 = $1.5 × 375 = **$562.50**

4. Price drops to $98.5

- New Delta ≈ -0.475 × 50 × 100 = -2375
- Hedge: Buy 500 shares (1875 → 2375) at $98.5
- **Profit:** Sold at $100.5, Bought at $98.5 = $2 × 375 = $750

5. Price returns to $100

- New Delta ≈ -0.40 × 50 × 100 = -2000
- Hedge: Sell 375 shares (2375 → 2000) at $100
- **Profit:** Bought at $98.5, Sold at $100 = $1.5 × 375 = **$562.50**

Price Move	Shares Adjusted	Profit
$100 → $101	-250	$250
$101 → $99	+500	$500
$99 → $100.5	-375	$562.50
$100.5 → $98.5	+500	$750
$98.5 → $100	-375	$562.50
Total	—	**$2,625**

C. Gamma Scalping Set Ups Using TradeStation Tools

The calculations in the above examples were made simple because the delta and gamma shown were manipulated slightly to make the example easier to understand. In real life trades this can be harder. Luckily, we can use our trading platform to do the hard work for us. Let's look at a couple of examples:

Example 1 with Puts and Stock: A Computer Hardware company's stock is trading at 27.89. First, we look at the single options that are ATM and about 6 months before expiration. We find that the November 28 puts have a Delta of -0.42 and a Gamma of 0.048.

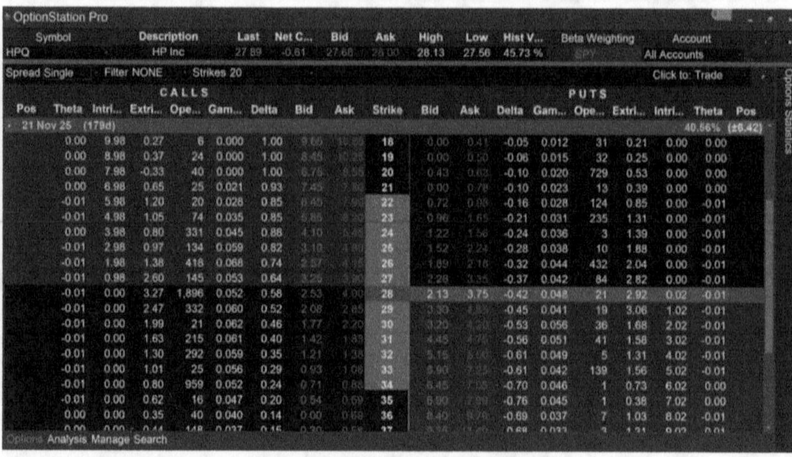
OptionStation Pro

Symbol	Description	Last	Net C...	Bid	Ask	High	Low	Hist V...	Beta Weighting	Account
HPQ	HP Inc	27.89	-0.61	27.68	28.00	28.13	27.56	45.73 %	SPY	All Accounts

Spread Single · Filter NONE · Strikes 20 · Click to: Trade

21 Nov 25 (179d) · 40.56% (±6.42)

Pos	Theta	Intri...	Extri...	Ope...	Gam...	Delta	Bid	Ask	Strike	Bid	Ask	Delta	Gam...	Ope...	Extri...	Intri...	Theta	Pos
CALLS										PUTS								
	0.00	9.98	0.27	6	0.000	1.00	[illegible]	[illegible]	18	0.00	0.41	-0.05	0.012	31	0.21	0.00	0.00	
	0.00	8.98	0.37	24	0.000	1.00	8.45	10.25	19	0.00	0.50	-0.06	0.015	32	0.25	0.00	0.00	
	0.00	7.98	-0.33	40	0.000	1.00	6.75	[illegible]	20	0.43	[illegible]	-0.10	0.020	729	0.53	0.00	0.00	
	0.00	6.98	0.65	25	0.021	0.93	7.45	[illegible]	21	0.00	0.78	-0.10	0.023	13	0.39	0.00	0.00	
	-0.01	5.98	1.20	20	0.028	0.85	[illegible]	[illegible]	22	0.72	[illegible]	-0.16	0.028	124	0.85	0.00	-0.01	
	-0.01	4.98	1.05	74	0.035	0.85	[illegible]	[illegible]	23	0.96	1.65	-0.21	0.031	235	1.31	0.00	-0.01	
	0.00	3.98	0.80	331	0.045	0.88	4.10	[illegible]	24	1.22	1.56	-0.24	0.036	3	1.39	0.00	-0.01	
	-0.01	2.98	0.97	134	0.059	0.82	3.10	[illegible]	25	1.52	2.24	-0.28	0.038	10	1.88	0.00	-0.01	
	-0.01	1.98	1.38	418	0.068	0.74	[illegible]	[illegible]	26	1.89	2.16	-0.32	0.044	432	2.04	0.00	-0.01	
	-0.01	0.98	2.60	145	0.053	0.64	3.25	[illegible]	27	2.28	3.35	-0.37	0.042	84	2.82	0.00	-0.01	
	-0.01	0.00	3.27	1,896	0.052	0.58	2.53	4.00	28	2.13	3.75	-0.42	0.048	21	2.92	0.02	-0.01	
	-0.01	0.00	2.47	332	0.060	0.52	2.08	2.65	29	3.30	[illegible]	-0.45	0.041	19	3.06	1.02	-0.01	
	-0.01	0.00	1.99	21	0.062	0.46	1.77	2.20	30	3.20	[illegible]	-0.53	0.056	36	1.68	2.02	-0.01	
	-0.01	0.00	1.63	215	0.061	0.40	1.42	1.83	31	4.45	[illegible]	-0.56	0.051	41	1.58	3.02	-0.01	
	-0.01	0.00	1.30	292	0.059	0.35	1.21	1.38	32	5.15	[illegible]	-0.61	0.049	5	1.31	4.02	-0.01	
	-0.01	0.00	1.01	25	0.056	0.29	0.93	1.08	33	5.90	[illegible]	-0.61	0.042	139	1.56	5.02	-0.01	
	-0.01	0.00	0.80	959	0.052	0.24	0.71	0.88	34	6.45	[illegible]	-0.70	0.046	1	0.73	6.02	0.00	
	-0.01	0.00	0.62	16	0.047	0.20	0.54	0.69	35	6.90	[illegible]	-0.76	0.045	1	0.38	7.02	0.00	
	0.00	0.00	0.35	40	0.040	0.14	0.00	0.69	36	8.40	[illegible]	-0.69	0.037	7	1.03	8.02	-0.01	

Options Analysis Manage Search

We also find that if we use the TradeStation OptionStation platform's Spread Cover/Married Stock selection category we can find a combination of puts and stocks that gives us a very close to Delta Neutral position by buying 50 puts and 2077 shares of stock. From the below Screenshot of the platform, we can also see that the total Theta for this combination of puts and Stock is -35.53. This means that just having this position in place will cost the trader $35.53 per day in decay of the puts.

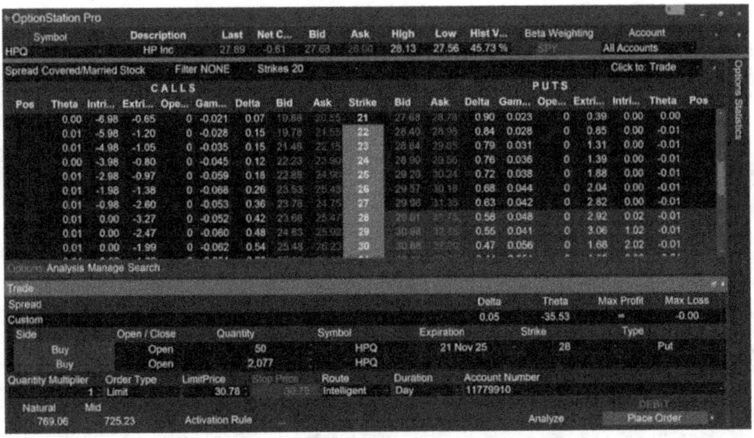

If you assume that the put mid-price is about $2.9, the total cost for this set up is:

Long Put Costs: 50 x $2.9 x 100 = $14,500

Stock Costs: $27.89 x 2077 = $57,927

Total Costs = $72,427

Now let's look a less expensive set up for a similar

Example 2 with Puts and Calls: A Computer Hardware company's stock is trading at 27.89. First, we look at the single options that are ATM and about 6 months before expiration. We find that the November 28 puts have a Delta of -0.42 and a Gamma of 0.048, and that the November 28 calls have a Delta of 0.52 and a Gamma of 0.052.

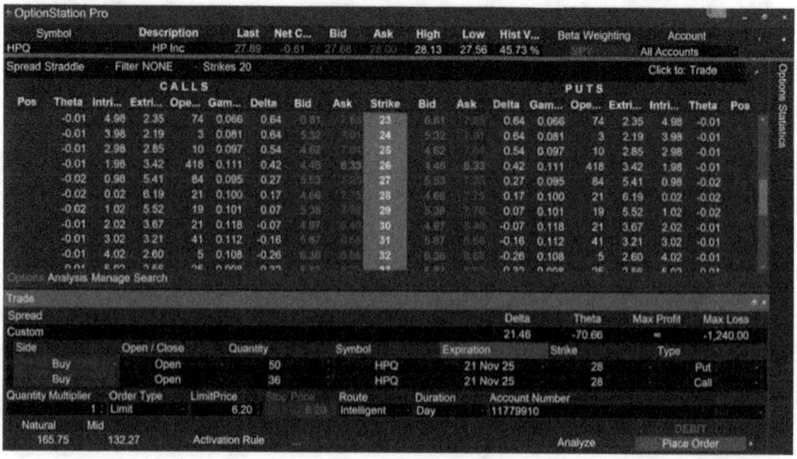

We also find that if we use the TradeStation OptionStation platform's Straddle selection category, we can find a combination of puts and calls that gives us a very close to Delta Neutral position by buying 50 puts and 36 calls. From this Screenshot of the platform, we can also see that the total Theta for this combination of puts and Stock is -70.66. This means that just having this position in place will cost the trader $70.66 per day in decay of the puts and calls.

If you assume that the put mid-price is about $2.9 and the call mid-price is $3.25 the total cost for this set up is:

Long Put Costs: 50 x $2.9 x 100 = $14,500

Long Calls Costs: 36 x $3.25 x 100 = $11,700

Total Costs = $26,200

D. Selecting Stocks for Gamma Scalping

Over several years of Gamma Scalping, I have identified a number of Stocks that I like to use, but I still perform an analysis every time to make sure that the criteria that I like are met before opening an initial position. I also use a Firebird search tool, which has built-in criteria that is used to find Gamma Scalping stocks. Here is a look at this Firebird tool.

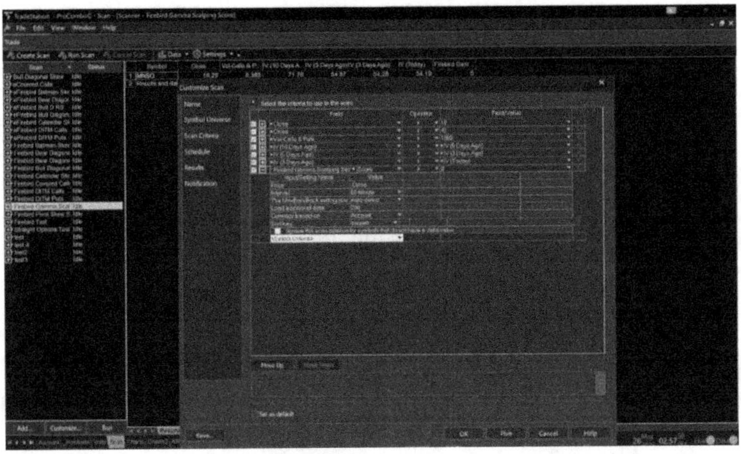

This Screenshot shows the initial set up for the tool. I like stocks in a lower price range. In this case between 10 and 42 dollars per share and IV that has been decreasing recently.

Of course, to determine if the stock that was found by this search is a good candidate for Gamma Scalping a full analysis would need to be performed by looking at the option prices, Deltas, and Gammas, as we did previously.

Conclusion

These examples illustrate that gamma scalping is not about predicting market direction—it's about responding to it. Rather than attempting to forecast whether a stock will rise or fall, gamma scalpers capitalize on movement itself. Every oscillation in price, every reversion to the mean, becomes a monetizable moment.

What makes this strategy powerful is its **mechanical nature**. It removes emotional decision-making by replacing it with a defined process: monitor delta, rebalance with stock, repeat.

The Power of Repetition

- **Example:** Multiple rebalances resulted in significant realized profits.
- Micro-profits accumulate over time and can compound across days or weeks, especially in high-volatility regimes.

Strategic Advantages Recap:

- **Delta-neutral foundation** minimizes directional exposure.
- **Gamma sensitivity** ensures that each price move produces a tradable signal.
- **Volatility** amplifies delta changes and expands range of opportunity.
- **Risk management** is built in—positions are constantly adjusted to remain balanced.

This is why gamma scalping is a favored tactic for advanced traders who want to turn uncertainty into opportunity. It's a proactive, adaptive approach suited for fast-moving environments, intraday reversals, and stocks with high liquidity.

Up Next: In the next chapter, we'll explore the **technical analysis tools** that help gamma scalpers enhance their edge—tools that:

- Time scalping entries around expected volatility spikes
- Spot pivot zones for likely reversals
- Use momentum indicators to guide when to scale in or pull back

You'll learn how to combine these tools with the Greeks to reinforce every decision—so your campaign becomes smarter, tighter, and more profitable with every adjustment.

Chapter: 9

Technical Analysis in Volatile Markets

Volatile markets challenge every trader's conviction, timing, and discipline. In these high-velocity environments, **Technical Analysis (TA)** becomes a powerful decision-making framework—not just for entries and exits, but for managing trade structure and adjusting campaign positions. This chapter focuses on the TA tools that work best when volatility runs high and markets are reactive.

Which Indicators Work Best in Unstable Environments

Not all technical indicators are equally effective in volatile markets. Some lag or provide conflicting signals. The most useful tools in unstable environments are those that:

- React to price expansion in real time
- Adapt to increased trading ranges
- Help define levels of exhaustion, reversion, or breakout potential

Here are the core indicators every campaign trader should consider:

Average True Range (ATR)

- ATR measures the average range of price movement over a defined number of periods (e.g., 14 days). • Rising ATR indicates expanding volatility, while falling ATR suggests consolidation.

Use ATR to:

- **Size trades** appropriately by scaling stops and position sizes to reflect volatility
- **Time gamma scalping:** Enter positions when ATR reaches recent highs—signaling optimal reversion setups

Example: If ATR on SPY jumps from 3 to 6, expect larger intraday swings and plan for more frequent scalping adjustments or wider spread strikes.

Bollinger Bands

- Composed of a moving average (typically 20-day SMA) and two outer bands set 2 standard deviations away. • As volatility rises, the bands expand; as it contracts, they tighten.

Use Cases:

- **Mean reversion trades** when price pierces outside the bands, especially on low volume
- **Momentum breakout entries** when bands expand alongside volume

Example: When an EV stock breaks above its upper Bollinger Band with strong volume and momentum, it often continues 3–5% before reverting—ideal for short-term directional legs.

RSI Divergence (Relative Strength Index)

- RSI measures momentum, typically on a 14-period basis. Readings above 70 are considered overbought, below 30 oversold. •
- **Divergence** occurs when price makes new highs/lows, but RSI fails to follow.

Use for:

- Spotting potential reversal points near pivot zones
- Timing adjustments for diagonal spreads or verticals

Example: If an AI Semiconductor stock makes a new high but RSI peaks lower than the previous high, traders might close bullish diagonals or roll short legs higher.

MACD Crossovers

- The Moving Average Convergence Divergence (MACD) tracks the relationship between two EMAs (12 and 26 by default) and the 9-period signal line. • Crossovers above/below the signal line indicate momentum shifts.

Best Used For:

- Confirming directional conviction before layering or adjusting trades

- Timing pivot-based reversals or trend extensions

Example: After a hard sell-off, a MACD bullish crossover on a Smartphone Manufacturing stock could confirm a short-term bounce—ideal for adding bullish diagonals or adjusting put spreads.

These indicators are tools to refine—not replace—your options decisions. When used together with volatility analysis, pivot zones, and Greek awareness, they become part of a comprehensive decision-making framework that supports both entry and adjustment timing.

Volume Profile and VWAP in Intraday Volatility

Volume-based analysis is invaluable when volatility distorts typical technical patterns.

Volume Profile

- Shows where the most trading occurred over a price range.
- Use high-volume nodes (HVNs) as support/resistance zones.
- Low-volume nodes (LVNs) often produce fast moves (price skips).

VWAP (Volume Weighted Average Price)

- Institutional benchmark for fair value.
- In volatile markets:
  - Longs above VWAP are strong
  - Shorts below VWAP are favored
  - Crossing VWAP with volume confirms sentiment shifts

Integrate VWAP into:

- Intraday gamma scalping triggers
- Add-on trades within a diagonal campaign

Entry/exit filter in scalping or income strategies

Price Action Around Pivot Zones and Psychological Levels

Price has memory—especially around pivot zones and psychological round numbers (e.g., 100, 200, 300). In volatile markets, these levels often act as magnetic points where price stalls, reverses, or accelerates.

Use these zones to:

- Stage diagonal spreads with offset strikes
- Trigger rebalancing in gamma scalping (as price breaks or rejects levels)
- Manage campaign exits or adjustment branches

Watch for:

- Pin bars and engulfing candles
- Breakout failures and false moves near pivots
- Volume confirmation when levels hold or break

How to Integrate TA into Entry/Exit and Adjustment Logic

The best traders use technical analysis not as a prediction tool, but as a framework for timing and confirmation.

Entry:

- Align TA signals (e.g., MACD cross, Bollinger squeeze, RSI divergence) with a volatility-based setup (e.g., IV Rank > 50, delta-neutral foundation).
- For example, when price compresses inside narrowing Bollinger Bands and RSI begins to diverge, a gamma scalp setup using ATM options with high gamma may be ideal.

Exit:

- Use resistance zones, psychological levels, or prior swing highs/lows to trim or close position legs.
- Monitor ATR or band compression to identify "end of move" conditions—signals to de-risk.
- For instance, after a rally reaches a volume shelf at $105 with fading MACD momentum, consider taking profit on directional legs.

Adjustments:

- Wait for confirmation near support/resistance before rolling or flipping spreads.

- Rebuild delta-neutral gamma positions after price stabilizes at a volume node or VWAP level.
- **Example:** If XYZ drops to a prior support node at $95 with RSI divergence and ATR spiking, that may be your signal to roll a short put higher in a diagonal or reduce short stock exposure in a gamma scalp.

Technical analysis is not about predicting direction—it's about timing trades and managing risk effectively. When used alongside volatility tools and the Greeks, TA provides campaign traders with a high-confidence playbook for volatile conditions.

In Summary

In volatile markets, **technical analysis (TA)** becomes more than just a visual tool or academic exercise—it becomes a **tactical compass** that guides your decision-making in real time. When prices move quickly and unpredictably, TA provides the structure and logic to help you stay focused, not flustered.

Used correctly, TA enables traders to:

- **Time entries** at key inflection points
- **Confirm volatility-based setups**
- **Trigger gamma adjustments** with confidence
- **Filter out noise** and prioritize high-probability opportunities

TA + Options Structure = Campaign Precision

Where traditional TA might simply identify trend or reversal opportunities, campaign traders apply TA as a **decision framework.** For example:

- A **Bollinger Band squeeze breakout** may signal the optimal moment to open a **long diagonal spread**, especially if supported by IV expansion and a rising ATR.
- **RSI divergence** near a key pivot level might trigger a **rebalancing action** in a gamma scalping campaign, where the trader closes or reverses part of their delta hedge.

- A **MACD crossover** post-earnings can confirm direction for adjusting a calendar spread into a directional diagonal or converting an iron condor into a ratio spread.

By **synchronizing TA signals with options positioning**, traders not only improve their edge—they also **gain clarity under pressure.**

Staying Grounded During Volatility

Volatile markets challenge emotional discipline. TA helps traders:

- **Define boundaries:** ATR bands and volume zones establish realistic expectations.
- **Reduce guesswork:** Patterns offer probabilistic confidence.
- **Execute faster:** Visual cues trigger timely adjustments without overthinking.

Example: Imagine you're managing a **gamma scalping position** on a tech stock that has ranged between $95 and $105. The price hits $105 with RSI diverging and volume drying up. Instead of chasing the move, you:

- Scale down your long gamma exposure
- Tighten your rebalancing threshold
- Prepare to flip the hedge if price breaks down through $103

Without TA, this adjustment would be reactive. With it, it's **strategic.**

Final Note

When paired with well-structured option strategies, **technical analysis transforms campaign trading into a dynamic, adaptable system**—not just a set-and-forget position. In volatile markets, this synergy gives traders the ability to:

Adjust with confidence

Read market signals faster

Stay consistent across shifting conditions

Chapter: 10

Deep-In-The-Money Calls and Puts – Precision Tools for Volatile Campaigns

A. Introduction to Deep-in-the-Money Options

In a market where speed, precision, and flexibility matter more than ever, deep-in-the-money (DITM) options emerge as one of the most tactical tools in a campaign trader's arsenal. These are not the flashy, lotto-ticket options that expire tomorrow. Instead, they are sturdy, high-confidence instruments that let traders express directional conviction with built-in risk management and capital efficiency.

1. What Are Deep-in-the-Money (DITM) Calls and Puts?

A **deep-in-the-money option** is one where the strike price is significantly below (for calls) or above (for puts) the current market price of the underlying stock. For example, if stock XYZ is trading at $120, a $90 call or a $150 put might be considered DITM. These options cost more than out-of-the-money (OTM) options because they already hold substantial intrinsic value—but they also come with advantages that campaign traders can exploit.

DITM Options as Stock Substitutes

The defining feature of DITM options is their **high delta,** usually in the range of **0.80 to 1.00**. This means that the price of a DITM call or put will move almost dollar-for-dollar with the underlying stock. As a result, they behave **very similarly to owning or shorting shares**, but with less capital at risk.

For instance, owning a DITM call with a delta of 0.95 on a $100 stock gives you nearly the same price exposure as owning 100 shares, but often with less than 40% of the capital outlay. This makes DITM options an attractive **leverage tool** for disciplined traders who want directional exposure without overcommitting capital.

B. Why DITM Works in Volatile Conditions

In highly volatile markets, DITM options offer several unique advantages:

- **Price Tracking Precision:** Because of their high delta, DITM options move closely with the stock. This allows for precise tracking in fast-moving conditions without the theta decay or volatility distortion that plagues at-the-money or OTM options.
- **Reduced Time Decay (Theta):** Since most of a DITM option's value is intrinsic, it is less affected by time decay. This is critical when a campaign may take several days or weeks to develop.
- **Lower Vega Sensitivity:** DITM options are less impacted by changes in implied volatility, which can otherwise disrupt profit/loss expectations during news events or market-wide IV shifts.
- **Defined Risk vs. Stock:** Buying a DITM call or put limits your downside to the premium paid—unlike owning stock outright, which exposes you to a full price drop.

1. When DITM Options Outperform

While not always the flashiest position, DITM options tend to outperform in several key scenarios:

High-Volatility, Directional Moves

- When traders expect a strong price move but want to avoid the slippage and spread risks of far OTM options.

Breakout Campaigns

- After confirmation of a bullish breakout, DITM calls can replace stock to gain exposure with lower capital and hedged risk.

Stock Substitution in Portfolio Hedging

- Rather than selling stock to manage risk, traders might use DITM puts to create controlled downside exposure.

Event-Driven Swings

- If earnings or macro news is anticipated and there's conviction in direction, DITM options allow participation with less gamma risk and more stable performance.

C. Campaign Trader's Perspective

For campaign traders, **DITM options offer flexibility across timelines.** They serve as effective building blocks for layering spreads, rolling diagonals, or staging exit legs as a campaign unfolds. In volatile environments—where reactivity and capital management define success—DITM options let you stay in the fight without overexposing your portfolio.

My use of DITM options is only under conditions where I have a very high confidence that the market and the underlying stock will make the directional move anticipated. Also, I always use Firebird tools and plan to be in and out of a position in days.

1. Risk/Reward Characteristics of DITM Options

Understanding the **risk and reward profile** of deep-in-the-money (DITM) options is critical to using them effectively within a campaign trading strategy. These options are engineered for precision—offering stock-like price participation with risk-defined characteristics and enhanced capital efficiency.

Delta-Driven Exposure with Defined Risk

The core appeal of DITM options lies in their **high delta**, typically ranging from **0.80 to nearly 1.00**. This means the option behaves almost like a share of stock—moving nearly dollar-for-dollar with the underlying.

But unlike stock, the risk is capped. If you purchase a DITM call or put, your **maximum loss is limited to the premium paid**. This provides traders with a powerful directional tool that comes pre-packaged with a protective floor.

Example: A DITM call with a 0.95 delta will gain roughly $0.95 for every $1 move up in the stock. But if the stock tanks, your loss is limited to what you paid—not the full drop.

Reduced Time Decay (Theta)

Unlike at-the-money (ATM) or out-of-the-money (OTM) options, DITM contracts derive most of their value from **intrinsic value** rather than time value. As a result, **theta decay**—the erosion of option value over time—is much less impactful.

This characteristic makes DITM options especially attractive for **multi-day or multi-week** campaigns, where a trader expects a move but doesn't want time decay to eat away their position if the move takes longer than anticipated.

A $10 DITM option may lose just a few cents a day in theta, while a $2 ATM option might lose 10–15 cents per day if volatility falls or the stock stagnates.

Lower Vega Sensitivity: A More Stable Play in IV Storms

Implied volatility (IV) has less impact on DITM options because their value is largely made up of intrinsic value. **Vega**, which measures sensitivity to changes in IV, is lower in DITM options than in ATM or OTM counterparts.

In high-IV environments—such as just before earnings or macro announcements—this provides insulation from sudden IV collapse. That makes DITM options an excellent tool for **traders who want exposure to price movement without being overly exposed to volatility swings.**

2. Capital Efficiency vs. Owning Stock

A major advantage of DITM options is their ability to **mimic stock exposure using far less capital.** Let's consider a practical example:

Practical Example: Buying a DITM $80 Call on XYZ Trading at $100

Trade Structure	Exposure	Capital Outlay	Breakeven	Risk	Leverage
Buy 100 shares at $100	$10,000	$10,000	$100	Full downside	1:1
Buy 1 DITM $80 Call for $22	~$9,500 (delta 0.95)	$2,200	$102	Max $2,200	~4.5:1

- **Exposure:** Nearly identical price tracking due to 0.95 delta.
- **Capital Efficiency:** ~78% less capital required.
- **Breakeven:** Slightly above the current price due to premium paid.
- **Downside Risk:** Limited to premium vs. full value of stock.

This example shows how a trader can get **almost full participation in upside** while limiting downside and dramatically reducing capital committed.

In Summary

DITM options offer a powerful blend of:

- Stock-like performance with defined risk
- Low exposure to time decay and volatility swings
- Efficient capital deployment

These characteristics make them ideal instruments for volatile environments, where traders want precision control without overexposure. Whether used as a standalone directional play or layered into a multi-leg campaign strategy, DITM options allow you to manage risk **on your terms.**

D. Technical Analysis to Guide DITM Entry

When trading Deep-in-the-Money (DITM) options, **timing is everything**. Because DITM options carry high delta and significant capital exposure, campaign traders must lean on **technical analysis (TA)** to select precise entries and confirm directional conviction. TA doesn't predict the future—but it gives you **structured confidence** in volatile conditions.

1. **Trend Confirmation Tools for Directional DITM Campaigns**

Before committing to a DITM position, traders should ensure the stock is exhibiting a **clear, strong directional trend**. Several chart-based tools can help validate this conviction:

Moving Averages (50/200 SMA Crossovers)

- A classic trend-following method.
- A **bullish crossover** (50-day SMA crossing above the 200-day) supports long DITM calls.
- A **bearish crossover** suggests potential for DITM puts.

Example: XYZ stock breaks above its 200-day SMA with a rising 50-day SMA. This confirms long-term momentum is turning bullish—a strong technical setup for entering a long DITM call.

MACD Crossovers (Moving Average Convergence Divergence)

- The MACD line crossing above the signal line provides additional momentum confirmation.
- Particularly useful when combined with a breakout from a consolidation or range.

Strategy Tip: Look for MACD confirmation within one to two sessions of your moving average crossover to reduce false signals.

ADX (Average Directional Index)

- Measures **trend strength**, not direction.
- ADX above 20–25 indicates that a **trend is developing.**
- Pair ADX with a directional tool (like MACD) to verify whether the trend is trade-worthy.

DITM Call Example: 50/200 SMA cross bullish, MACD cross confirmed, ADX rises above 25 — this trifecta is a strong case to scale into a DITM call campaign.

2. Support & Resistance: Where Price Meets Planning

DITM entries are most effective when placed near **clear technical support or resistance zones,** offering both conviction and defined risk points.

Pivot-Based Entry Zones

- Look for bounce points at prior swing highs/lows.
- Use Fibonacci retracements to find reactive zones (e.g., 38.2% or 61.8% levels).
- Enter DITM calls near **support pivots**, and DITM puts near **resistance pivots.**

Example: A stock pulls back to its 50-day SMA, which also aligns with a prior resistance turned support. Entering a DITM call here gives you defined technical support.

Volume Profile and VWAP Convergence

- Use **Volume Profile** to identify High Volume Nodes (HVNs)—price levels where institutional volume clusters.
- **Anchored VWAP** from earnings or major pivot points helps confirm institutional buying/selling zones.
- These zones are ideal for **DITM entries,** where traders can lean on both liquidity and conviction.

Visual Description: A chart of XYZ shows price bouncing off its 200-day SMA, which overlaps with a high-volume node and an anchored VWAP. This triple-confirmation makes an ideal launchpad for a DITM call.

E. Selecting the Right Strike and Expiration

Once you've confirmed the technical setup for a Deep-in-the-Money (DITM) trade, the next step is **structuring the trade with precision**. This includes choosing the **optimal strike price, expiration date,** and managing **liquidity and execution quality**—all of which influence profitability, capital efficiency, and adjustment flexibility.

1. Strike Price Positioning: How Far In-the-Money Is "Deep"?

The deeper you go in-the-money, the closer the **delta** gets to 1.0, meaning your option behaves more like stock. However, that comes at a price—higher cost per contract and lower leverage.

Here's a basic rule of thumb:

- **Moderately DITM (Delta ≈ 0.80–0.85):**
  - Offers good leverage and stock-like behavior.
  - Suitable for directional swing trades and mid-length campaigns.
- **Deep DITM (Delta ≈ 0.90–0.95):**
  - Moves nearly dollar-for-dollar with the stock.
  - Best for traders seeking precision with reduced volatility and theta risk.
- **Ultra-DITM (Delta > 0.95):**
  - High cost, minimal time value.
  - Acts like a stock replacement; good for conservative or covered-call overlays.

Example: XYZ stock is trading at $100

You're evaluating three call strikes:

- $85 Call (Delta ≈ 0.95)
- $90 Call (Delta ≈ 0.85)
- $95 Call (Delta ≈ 0.75)

If the stock rises to $105, all three benefit, but the $85 strike delivers the most consistent move while exposing the least to time decay.

2. Expiration Date Selection: Balancing Time vs. Cost

When selecting your DITM expiration:

- **Shorter-Dated Options (2–4 weeks):**
  - Lower upfront cost.
  - Faster theta decay (especially if there's IV contraction).
  - Good for short-term trades tied to specific events or TA triggers.
- **Mid-Term Expirations (30–90 days):**
  - Balance between cost and stability.
  - Ideal for campaign trades that may adjust, roll, or evolve.
- **Long-Term Expirations (LEAPS, 6–12 months):**
  - Minimal time decay.
  - More expensive but stable.
  - Used in synthetic long positions or long-term overlays.

Example: A $90 call expiring in 15 days may have $8.50 premium ($7 intrinsic + $1.50 time value), while the same strike expiring in 90 days might cost $13.00. The 15-day option has a sharper theta but less capital at risk.

3. Delta Targeting: Why 0.80–0.95 Hits the Sweet Spot

High-delta DITM options behave like stock, but they also:

- Respond predictably to directional moves.
- Are less impacted by changes in implied volatility (low Vega).
- Reduce slippage and mispricing during volatility swings.

A **delta of 0.80–0.95** gives traders:

- More control over their exposure.
- Easier modeling for risk and reward.
- Greater predictability in campaign adjustments.

Tip: Pair high-delta DITM calls with gamma scalping or trend campaigns; they act as reliable core components around which short-term trades can be layered.

4. **Liquidity and Bid/Ask Spread Considerations**

Deeper strikes often see thinner volume. This can lead to:

- Wider bid/ask spreads
- Poor fills
- Slippage during adjustments

Before committing, check:

- **Open interest:** Ensure it's healthy (typically >500 contracts).
- **Bid/ask spread:** Should be no more than $0.10–$0.30 for active underlyings.
- **Volume vs. Vega:** Thin DITM options may overreact to volatility shifts in illiquid names.

Pro Tip: Trade DITM options on **high-volume ETFs** or megacap stocks for better fills and lower execution friction.

F. Example Table: How Different DITM Strikes Respond to a $5 Stock Move

XYZ Stock Price: $100	Strike	Delta	Cost	$5 Stock Move Value Gain	Approx. ROI
	$85	0.95	$16	$4.75	29.7%
	$90	0.85	$12	$4.25	35.4%
	$95	0.75	$8	$3.75	46.9%

Takeaway: Deeper DITM = more consistent gains, but lower leverage. Balance delta and cost with trade duration and campaign goals.

Final Thought

The strike and expiration you choose are more than a starting point—they define how the trade behaves under pressure. A thoughtful DITM setup minimizes risk and maximizes control, especially when paired with technical structure and an adaptive campaign mindset.

Think of DITM options as **precision anchors**—they offer directional exposure, manageable risk, and the flexibility to evolve. Whether you're collecting income, hedging downside, or shaping your profit zone with spreads, the ability to **campaign around a DITM core** gives you the edge to stay active and adaptive in volatile conditions.

G. Exit and Adjustment Strategies

Deep-in-the-money options may start as stable, stock-like core positions—but like any tool in a campaign trader's arsenal, they must evolve as the market evolves. Whether the underlying stock trends strongly, stalls, or reverses, traders must know when to adjust, scale, or exit to lock in profits or control risk.

This section explores how to manage DITM calls and puts after entry, including **when to transform them into spreads**, how to **roll them strategically,** and how to use **technical analysis** as a guide for exits and evolution.

1. When to Convert a DITM Into a Vertical or Diagonal Spread

Holding a DITM call or put gives you high directional exposure—but as price moves in your favor, you can reduce risk and enhance yield by converting it into a spread:

Vertical Spread Conversion

As the underlying climbs (for DITM calls) or falls (for DITM puts), consider **selling a farther OTM option** against your DITM leg to cap upside while bringing in premium.

Example:

- **Original position:** Long DITM $80 Call (stock at $100)
- **Adjustment:** Sell $110 Call when stock hits $105–$108

This creates a **$80/$110 bull call spread**, locking in most of the remaining upside and reducing exposure to a pullback or IV crush.

Diagonal Spread Adjustment

If you want to continue holding the DITM leg but reduce theta risk or take advantage of front-month IV, sell a shorter-dated call instead (e.g., 30 days out).

Tactical Benefit: Diagonals allow for **ongoing premium collection** while keeping longer-term bullish or bearish exposure.

2. **Rolling DITM Legs as Trends Evolve**

Just like adjusting a vertical spread, you can **roll a DITM option up (or down)** as the stock moves to keep delta in the ideal range (0.80–0.95) and avoid deep capital lock-up.

Example:

- Stock moves from $100 → $110
- Your DITM $80 Call now behaves like stock (delta ≈ 1.00)
- Premium has little time value left

Roll Plan:

- Sell $80 Call for $31.00
- Buy $90 Call for $22.00
- Pocket the difference or reinvest it to extend the campaign

Now your delta is reset closer to 0.85, and you have more room to benefit from further upside without full stock-like exposure.

3. **Using Technical Analysis to Signal Exit or Adjustments**

TA tools aren't just for entries—they're powerful signals for **taking profits or making structural changes** to your trade.

Watch for:

- **RSI > 70 or < 30:** Signals potential exhaustion
- **MACD divergence:** When price makes higher highs but momentum stalls
- **Trendline breaks:** End of structure, often justifies scaling out
- **Volume drop-off:** Weakening conviction in the move

Campaigning Tip: If price hits your technical target but implied volatility remains high, consider converting the DITM position into a **calendar or diagonal** to collect time premium while protecting gains.

4. Delta Erosion and Premium Decay Near Expiration

As expiration nears, your DITM option starts behaving more like **pure intrinsic value** and less like a flexible option.

Key Considerations:

- **Delta reaches 1.00:** No further gamma benefit
- **Theta accelerates:** Even DITM options start losing time value quickly
- **Liquidity tightens:** Bid/ask spreads can widen unexpectedly

Action: Either exit entirely or roll out to a new expiration at a higher strike, keeping the structure responsive and capital-efficient.

Example: Rolling a DITM $80 Call as Stock Moves from $100 → $110

Stock Price	Position	Delta	Action	Benefit
$100	Long $80 Call	≈ 0.95	Initial Entry	High exposure, low cost
$105	Call gains $25+	≈ 0.98	Consider selling $110 Call	Lock in premium, shape profit
$110	$80 Call deep ITM	≈ 1.00	Roll to $90 Call	Reset exposure, reduce capital

Managing DITM options is all about timing and precision. When used as part of a campaign strategy, these tools allow you to lock in gains, adapt exposure, and extend trades without overexposing capital.

Adjustment = Opportunity. When markets move fast, DITM options give you the **leverage of stock with the flexibility of structure.** Learn to manage the lifecycle, and they'll become one of your most powerful tools.

H. Finding and Analyzing DITM Options to Trade

Let's use the Firebird search tools to find some DITM Calls and then analyze them.

1. Using the TradeStation RadarScreen to find DITM Calls

The DITM Call search tool is set to search continuously once set up on the TradeStation RadarScreen.

Below is an example of this set up and also a chart that can be used for a quick evaluation of the stock.

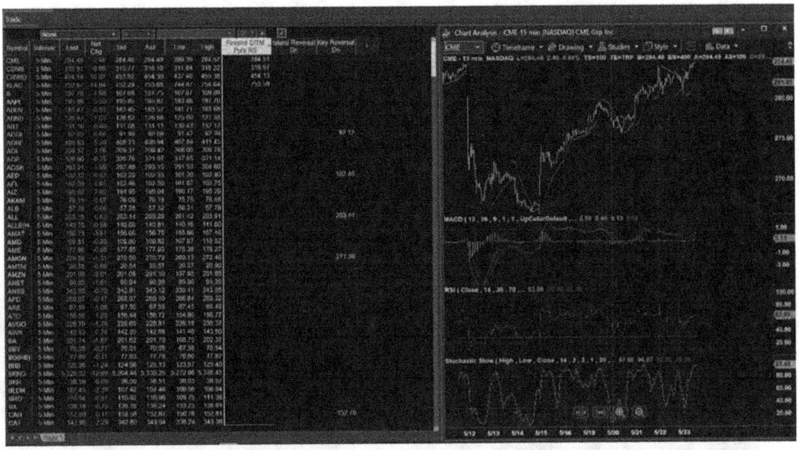

To see the stocks that have been found as potential good DITM calls candidates, you simply double click on the column heading. In the example, you see that 4 stocks have been found.

2. Using the TradeStation Scanner to find DITM Calls

This DITM Call search is manually initiated on the TradeStation Scanner.

Below is a Screenshot of an example of the results found.

TradeStation

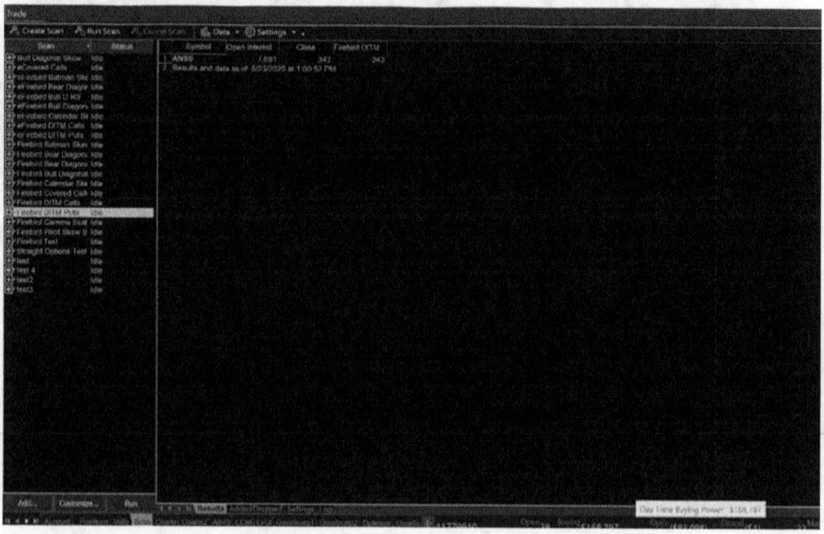

Below are results from another search performed later in the same day.

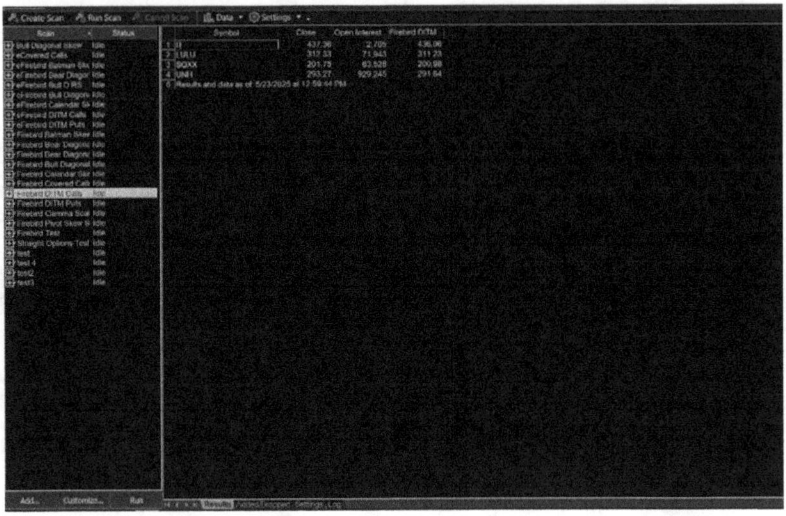

3. Technical Analysis of Stock Found

Once a potential stock is found technical analysis is performed to see if it is a good candidate.

15 Minute Chart

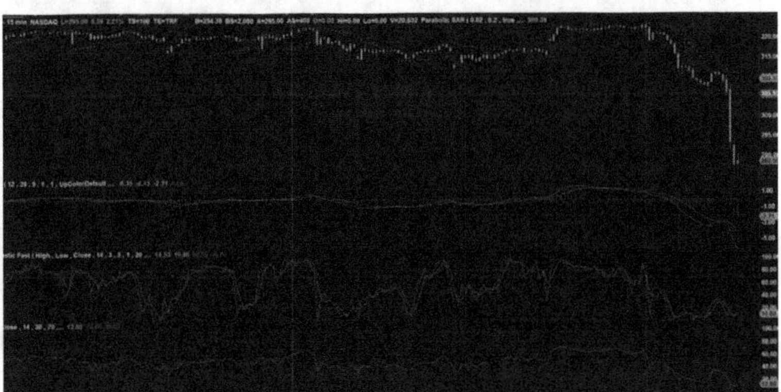

This 15-minute chart shows that the stock has bottomed out using several different analysis techniques. Now let's look at 5-minute chart.

5 Minute Chart

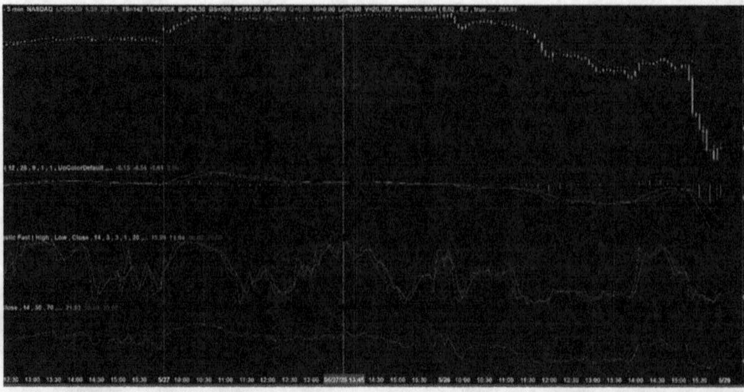

The 5-minute chart for this stock also still looks good and is looking like a good candidate at this point during the analysis.

1 Minute Chart

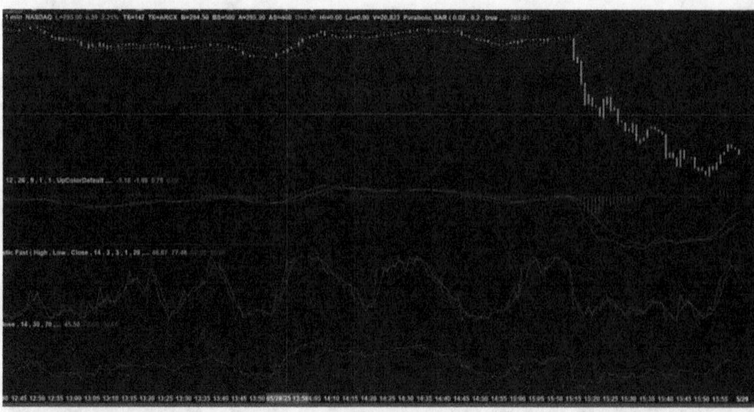

The 1-minute chart shows that we may need to wait for an entry. If the stock pulls back to the previous low in this timeframe or if the

Stochastics bottoms and begins to move back up that may be a good entry point.

4. Selecting the Call

The DITM call is analyzed in the TradeStation OptionStation platform.

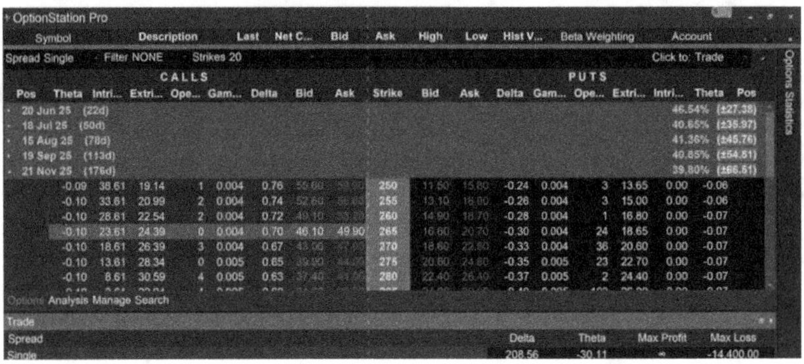

The stock is trading at 294.84. If we select a DITM November 265 call (6 months from expiration), it has these characteristics:

Price: about 48 mid-point, so it would cost ~$4800 to buy a single call.

Delta: 0.70

Gamma: 0.004

Theta: -0.10

Intrinsic Value: 23.61

If a trader did decide to invest in this DITM call it would be best to set a limit order that would be lower than the mid-point and at approximately where the price of the option would be if the underlying stock returned to the lowest point on the 1-minute chart.

If the limit order was not executed in a reasonable time, the trader could decide if he wanted to raise his entry limit price.

Conclusion: Deep-in-the-Money Options – Precision in Volatility

Deep-in-the-Money (DITM) calls and puts are more than just high-delta instruments—they are precision tools for campaign traders operating in volatile markets. Offering stock-like exposure with reduced capital outlay and greater flexibility than traditional spreads, DITM options allow traders to express directional bias with control, manage risk efficiently, and adapt quickly as trends evolve.

While they are not risk-free, the built-in advantages of high delta, reduced theta decay, and limited vega sensitivity make DITM options ideal for traders who value responsiveness over speculation. Whether used alone or as part of a layered strategy, DITM options reward preparation, discipline, and timing.

In a world where volatility favors the prepared, DITM options give you the edge to move with confidence—precisely, efficiently, and strategically.

Chapter: 11

Final Thoughts on Trading in Volatile Markets

Volatile markets are not anomalies—they're recurring features of modern finance. While many traders fear turbulence, campaign traders see it as an opportunity. Throughout this book, we've explored the strategies, techniques, and tools that allow traders to navigate uncertainty with clarity and precision. This final chapter brings it all together and provides guidance on turning knowledge into long-term mastery.

A. Summary of Key Techniques and Principles

The tools and techniques discussed throughout this book are not designed to be used in isolation—they form a modular, adaptive system. Campaign trading is about stitching these parts together in real-time to respond, adjust, and exploit opportunity as market conditions shift.

Let's recap the core principles and how they come to life in practical scenarios:

Volatility Is a Signal—Not a Stop Sign

Inexperienced traders often retreat when volatility rises. But campaign traders know that elevated implied volatility (IV) is often the entry bell for advanced strategies.

- **Example:** When IV Rank on SPY hits 80%, iron condors or calendar spreads can be deployed to collect premium from inflated options prices.
- During a Fed week, rather than avoiding the market, traders can set up short-term diagonals to capture IV contraction post-announcement.
- **Lesson:** Volatility isn't chaos—it's fuel. Treat it as a strategic trigger.

The Greeks Are Your Compass

Options Greeks provide the quantitative pulse of your positions.

- Delta shows directional exposure.
- Gamma signals how rapidly delta will change—key for scalping and rebalancing.
- Theta highlights time decay and tells you when premium is eroding.
- Vega helps manage exposure to changing volatility levels.
- Rho becomes important in long-dated trades or shifting rate environments.

Example: A trader holding a diagonal spread may shift short strikes to manage increasing delta and decreasing vega, especially if the underlying rallies into resistance.

Lesson: Don't guess—measure. Use Greeks as dashboards to drive decisions and adjustments.

Campaign-Style Thinking

Trading is not a single-entry game. Campaign-style traders:

- Enter flexibly with room to adjust.
- Layer positions over time (e.g., laddered diagonals or rolled calendars).
- Map out alternatives to pre-define responses to price, volatility, or event changes.

Example: Instead of closing a position when price nears a short strike, a trader rolls the short leg forward while holding the long—collecting more credit and extending the opportunity window.

Lesson: Think in branches, not dots. Every trade is a starting point for a managed campaign—not a binary win/loss outcome.

Gamma Scalping: Movement as a Monetization Engine

Rather than speculating on direction, gamma scalping allows you to monetize movement.

- **Start with a delta-neutral ATM position**
- **Adjust by buying low, selling high in the stock**
- **Hedge as delta shifts—harvesting profits each time**

Example: With XYZ at $100, a trader scalps gamma by holding 5 long calls and rebalancing shares as the price whips between $98 and $102, profiting from each re-hedge.

Lesson: Gamma scalping thrives when others panic. It's the strategy for those who don't need to be right—just fast and precise.

TA and Volatility Tools for Precision Timing

Trading without timing is like sailing without navigation. Technical analysis + volatility metrics give you the tools to:

- Enter after breakout confirmation or reversal patterns
- Adjust near pivot zones with volume profile or RSI divergence
- Exit when conditions shift—ATR compresses, momentum dies, or IV collapses

Example: A campaign trader waits for MACD crossover and Bollinger expansion before adding a leg to a long calendar trade. As ATR begins to decline, they prepare to reduce exposure.

Lesson: Combine pattern recognition with probability structure to trade with confidence, not emotion.

Final Insight: Mastery Is a Blend of Tools, Timing, and Temperament

Becoming a successful campaign trader is not just about memorizing tactics. It's about:

- Staying flexible in strategy, but rigid in discipline.
- Combining quantifiable metrics (the Greeks) with chart context and trade logic.

- Practicing, journaling, and improving, even when the trades don't go as planned.

Every market condition teaches something new. And in a volatility-driven world, the traders who thrive are not those who predict best—but those who adapt quickest.

B. Developing Your Personal Trade Selection and Adjustment Process

Campaign trading is not a one-size-fits-all system. It's a customizable framework that evolves as traders gain experience, build intuition, and refine their execution. The goal is to develop a personal playbook—a repeatable routine that adapts to volatility and capitalizes on market structure.

Below is a suggested blueprint that can be tailored over time to fit your trading style, account size, risk tolerance, and market engagement level.

1. Pre-Market Planning

Your edge starts before the bell rings. Each trading day begins with intentional screening and scenario-building.

Steps:

- **Scan for Candidates:**
  - Use volatility filters (IV Rank > 50%) and technical screens (e.g., RSI < 30 or > 70, Bollinger Band squeezes).
  - Look for stocks showing consistent intraday range expansion (e.g., ATR > 1.5% of price).
  - Prioritize high-liquidity stocks.
- **Identify Pivot Zones:**
  - Mark historical support/resistance levels, volume profile peaks, or psychological round numbers (e.g., \$100, \$150).
- **Evaluate IV Rank and Greek Profiles:**
  - Is implied volatility overpriced or underpriced?

- Use this insight to determine whether you'll be selling or buying premium.

- **Example:** If IV Rank is 85% and realized volatility is compressing, consider premium-selling diagonals near a pivot.

2. Initial Entry

Once trade candidates are selected, the next step is to establish a position with both strategic intent and built-in flexibility.

Steps:

- **Match Bias to Structure:**
  - **Bullish Bias:** Use a bull call diagonal or long call + short put spread.
  - **Neutral Bias:** Favor calendar spreads or iron condors around the expected range.
  - **Bearish Bias:** Use a bear put diagonal or long puts with gamma exposure.
- **Plan Adjustment Branches:**
  - Use decision trees or flowcharts to sketch out possible price paths and volatility outcomes.
  - **Example:** "If price breaks above resistance + IV drops → roll short strike higher and closer to expiry."
- **Define Hedging Points:**
  - For gamma scalping, decide when to rebalance delta (e.g., every 50 delta shift).
  - For spreads, predetermine theta thresholds (e.g., close if time value drops below 15%).

3. Live Management

Real-time monitoring and active response are essential to campaign-style trading.

Steps:

- **Track Greeks Continuously:**
  - Use platforms like TradeStation to view net delta, gamma, and theta in real-time.
  - If delta grows too directional, trim or hedge using micro-lots of stock or opposite options.
- **Rebalance Proactively:**
  - Example: If long 5 ATM calls with delta +250, and price jumps $1, gamma increases delta to +300 → Sell 50 shares to re-neutralize.
  - In a downward move, you'd buy back the shares to stay centered.
- **Use TA to Validate Adjustments:**
  - If price approaches a pivot zone with RSI divergence and ATR spike, use this technical confluence as confirmation to roll or scale the position.

4. Exit or Convert

No campaign lasts forever. The endgame is either a strategic exit or a conversion into a new phase.

Steps:

- **Exit the Position:**
  - If IV collapses or price exits the expected range, close the position or take profits on short legs.
  - **Example:** Gamma scalper who captured multiple hedge profits sees ATR drop—time to sell the long option and exit.
- **Convert the Campaign:**
  - If trend continues, roll short strikes and extend duration.
- **Manage Theta and Range:**
  - If theta erosion accelerates and price stalls, trim exposure or close legs.

- Use visual alerts like theta decay cones or time/value graphs to guide exits.

Key Takeaway

Your personal process is your edge amplifier. By blending volatility metrics, Greeks, and technical signals with a structured entry-and-adjustment framework, you move from reactive trading to campaign execution.

Over time, patterns will emerge in your journals:

- Which setups work best in certain IV conditions?
- When does rebalancing deliver the most profit?
- Which exits protect gains vs. which allow overstaying?

These answers become your playbook. And with each campaign, you fine-tune your edge.

C. Staying Focused, Adaptive, and Psychologically Strong

Volatility doesn't just test your strategy—it tests your mindset. In campaign trading, it's not the market's chaos that derails traders, but their emotional response to that chaos. Success lies in cultivating the mental discipline to stay centered, adaptable, and composed, no matter how wild the price swings get.

Focused: Execute Your Plan, Not Your Emotions

In a volatile session, price may rally sharply one moment and collapse the next. News hits, rumors fly, and volatility spikes without warning. In these moments, chasing movement or second-guessing your trade thesis can lead to unplanned losses and breakdowns in strategy execution.

Example: You've built a diagonal spread on an EV Manufacturing stock expecting sideways movement between $220 and $230. Mid-session, a sudden price drop to $215 causes a spike in volatility. Rather than panic and exit prematurely, you review your decision tree: the short strike is safe, gamma is manageable, and IV just created a better opportunity to roll. You remain calm—and even improve the position.

How to Stay Focused:

- Use written trade plans for each campaign including adjustment triggers.
- Set pre-defined alert zones (e.g., delta > +30) to cue action, not emotion.
- Avoid over-monitoring. Watching every tick can tempt reactionary trading.

Adaptive: Evolve With the Market, Not Against It

The best campaign traders don't marry their positions—they monitor evolving volatility, order flow, and technical structure to shift tactics on demand.

Markets rarely follow the script. The diagonal you initiated may need to become a ratio spread. A gamma scalp may need to pause if liquidity dries up. The key is responsiveness without emotional interference.

Example: You're long a calendar spread at the $190 strike. Volatility drops sharply post-event, compressing the back-month leg. The calendar no longer offers edge. You roll into a vertical debit spread, reduce size, and preserve capital—all because you didn't cling to a static plan.

Calm Under Fire: Master Your Emotions Before the Market Masters You

In fast markets, fear, frustration, or greed can override logic. Campaign traders need conviction in process, not the illusion of predicting every move.

Staying calm under pressure allows for objective assessment and prevents reactive errors. This is especially important when gamma exposure is high and hedging decisions must be made quickly and clearly.

Example: Your gamma scalp position in a volatile stock swings net delta from -100 to +100 within 20 minutes due to a rapid bounce. An emotional trader might freeze—or overtrade. But you've rehearsed the adjustment thresholds. You calmly execute two hedge trades and capture $1.30/share profit through volatility, because you followed the plan—not the fear.

How to Build Emotional Resilience:

- Journal trades daily—not just the results, but how you felt and reacted.
- Use checklists during rebalancing or position rollouts.
- Deploy AI tools (e.g., ChatGPT) to model scenarios in advance and avoid analysis paralysis during live action.

Mental clarity is your most underrated trading edge. The more systematic your thinking, the more confident your execution—and the more consistent your results.

In the next section, we'll walk through how continuous learning and journaling transforms short-term wins into long-term mastery.

E. Continuous Learning and Journaling as Part of Mastery

Mastery in campaign trading—especially in volatile markets—is not the result of one perfect trade, but the cumulative insight gained from repeated experience, disciplined reflection, and a mindset of continuous growth. Every trade teaches a lesson. The key is learning to hear it.

Why Journaling Matters

Keeping a detailed trading journal is like having a roadmap to your evolution as a trader. Without it, you're relying on vague memories and feelings. With it, you're capturing cause and effect, seeing patterns in behavior, and exposing both strengths and blind spots.

What to Include in a Trading Journal:

- **Trade Setup:** What did you enter, when, and why? What was the strategy and volatility context?
- **Greeks Snapshot:** Delta, Gamma, Theta, Vega at entry—and any significant shift points.
- **Adjustment Logic:** Why did you roll, hedge, or scale? What signals or data triggered it?
- **Emotional Notes:** How did you feel when price moved against you? Did you stick to the plan?

- **Outcome & Lessons:** Profit/loss is important—but the takeaway is more valuable. Did the trade go according to plan? What would you do differently?

Example Entry: Gamma Scalping Log

- **Date:** October 12
- **Stock:** trading at $440
- **Setup:** Bought 10 ATM weekly calls (Delta = +500), hedged with 500 short shares. IV Rank = 72%
- **Adjustment #1:** Stock rose to $444, delta shifted to +550. Sold 50 more shares.
- **Adjustment #2:** Dropped to $438, delta fell to +420. Bought 130 shares back.
- **Outcome:** $340 net gain from stock rebalancing. Closed options next day at small loss.
- **Reflection:** Managed emotions well, followed pre-planned delta rebalance rules. Rebalancing was timely. Theta loss minimized by exit timing.
- **Next Step:** Consider scaling down in similar IV environments—was slightly overexposed for account size.

Post-Trade Review: A Campaign Trader's Secret Weapon

Weekly or monthly trade reviews create compounding insight. Set aside time to:

- Analyze your most profitable trades—what common elements existed?
- Review losses for missed signals, late adjustments, or overtrading tendencies.
- Ask: What did I learn? What should I test or change next time?

This is how you move from execution to refinement, and from setups to systems.

Refining Your Personal Playbook

As markets change, so should your tactics. Campaign traders keep a living document that evolves based on performance data and pattern recognition.

Additions Might Include:

- New adjustment trees for diagonal spreads during earnings season.
- Adjusted delta thresholds for rebalancing gamma scalps in high-IV environments.
- Removing a spread setup that underperforms during low-liquidity Fridays.

Example: After tracking 15 backspread trades during high IV regimes, you realize your win rate improves significantly when using an IV Rank filter > 60%. You update your campaign rules to only deploy backspreads when IV Rank > 60% and RV > IV.

Ongoing Education: Keep Your Edge Sharp

The best traders aren't just traders—they're students of the market. In volatile environments, new edges and inefficiencies arise constantly.

Ways to Keep Learning:

- Subscribe to advanced options and volatility research.
- Use tools like ChatGPT to summarize macroeconomic shifts or test strategy logic.
- Join trader groups or mentoring circles to share adjustments and see others' trade.
- Attend live webinars, conferences, or roundtables.

Tip: Automate Learning With AI

Use AI to help analyze your journal. Feed in your entries and ask for patterns in decision-making, missed signals, or bias. AI can help optimize your feedback loop.

Campaign trading is more than strategy—it's a discipline of refinement. Journaling and continuous learning turn daily trades into compounding skill. It's the quiet edge most traders ignore, but one that separates the good from the great.

Final Thoughts: Trading with Precision in a World of Uncertainty

In volatile markets, the unprepared panic.

The strategic adjust.

Volatility can be overwhelming to those without a plan. The whipsaws, the news-driven gaps, the rising and falling tides of sentiment—it all seems unpredictable. But for the campaign trader, volatility is not chaos; it's structure in motion. It's fuel.

This book was written to equip you not just with tactics, but with a framework. You've learned how to:

- Identify volatility regimes and align them with your trading approach
- Measure and manage risk using the Greeks, IV metrics, and option sensitivity
- Construct adaptive spreads, like diagonals and calendars, near key pivot zones
- Implement gamma scalping to harvest movement instead of fearing it
- Blend technical and volatility analysis for precise entries and intelligent adjustments
- Record, refine, and grow using journaling and review processes

Campaign trading is not about making perfect calls. It's about building structures that evolve, knowing how and when to adjust, and using volatility not as a threat, but as an engine for profit.

Now It's Your Turn to Build the Playbook

Every successful options trader eventually develops a personal system. A way to scan for trades, construct positions, and respond to changing market dynamics. This book was the blueprint. Your next step is to build upon it:

- Draft your checklists and playbooks
- Create decision trees that guide adjustments under pressure
- Record your trades, study your missteps, and refine with discipline
- Keep a volatility dashboard—watching IV Rank, expected move models, and real-time Greeks

You now understand what most traders never do: how to trade not in spite of volatility—but because of it.

Volatility Is No Longer the Enemy. It's the Edge.

Every price spike, every volatility event, every earnings surprise is a moment of leverage for the prepared trader.

While others flinch, you adapt.

While others wait, you prepare.

While others guess, you build structure.

Thank You for Joining the Journey

If you've made it to this point, you've proven that you're committed to more than luck or hype. You're committed to craft. Campaign trading is one of the most advanced forms of market engagement—but also one of the most rewarding.

Now it's time to:

Build your playbook

Trade your campaign

Trust your preparation

Evolve with the market

Go trade with Confidence and Resolve.

Firebird Trading Systems Mission Statement:

At Firebird Trading Systems, our mission is to empower traders at every level—whether you're just starting or looking to refine your skills—by providing cutting-edge, fully automated trading systems and powerful tools for stocks, futures, forex, cryptocurrencies, and options. Driven by a team of passionate developers, trainers, and support professionals, we are committed to delivering innovative solutions that enhance your trading experience, simplify and improve decision-making, and unlock new opportunities in the markets.

We believe in the power of technology to elevate trading success, and our purpose is to help new and intermediate traders confidently navigate complex markets, optimize their strategies, and achieve their financial goals. At Firebird, we don't just build tools—we build the future of trading.

Firebird Trading Systems

Appendices:

Appendix A

Firebird Trading Systems Products

Option Skew Search tools

https://firebirdtradingsystems.com/scanner-tools/

Stock Algo Trading Systems

https://firebirdtradingsystems.com/stock-algo-trading-systems/

Futures Algo Trading Systems

https://firebirdtradingsystems.com/futures-algo-trading-systems/

Forex Algo Trading Systems

https://firebirdtradingsystems.com/forex-algo-trading-systems/

Cryptocurrency ETF Algo Trading Systems

https://firebirdtradingsystems.com/crypto-etf-trading-systems/

Appendix B

Glossary of Option Trading Terms

Glossary of Option Trading Terms

A comprehensive list of option trading terms, including the Greeks, components of the Black-Scholes option valuation formula, security types with options, and types of options, each accompanied by a short description:

The Greeks

Delta: Measures the rate of change of the option's price relative to a one-unit change in the price of the underlying asset.

Gamma: Represents the rate of change in Delta for a one-unit change in the price of the underlying asset.

Theta: Indicates the rate of decline in the value of an option due to the passage of time.

Vega: Measures the sensitivity of the option's price to changes in the volatility of the underlying asset.

Rho: Represents the rate of change of the option's price relative to a change in the risk-free interest rate.

Black-Scholes Option Valuation Formula

The Black-Scholes equation, also known as the Black-Scholes-Merton model, is a fundamental concept in financial mathematics used for pricing European-style options. The model provides a theoretical estimate of the price of European-style options and is widely used in the financial industry.

The Black-Scholes model assumes that the price of the underlying asset follows a lognormal distribution and that the markets are frictionless (no transaction costs or taxes, and the ability to borrow and lend money at the risk-free rate). It also assumes no dividends are paid out to the underlying asset during the life of the option. Despite its simplifying assumptions, the Black-Scholes model remains one of the most important tools in financial option pricing.

Spot Price (S): The current price of the underlying asset.

Strike Price (K): The price at which the option holder can buy (call) or sell (put) the underlying asset.

Time to Expiration (T): The time remaining until the option's expiration date, usually in years.

Volatility (σ): The annualized standard deviation of the underlying asset's returns, representing its price variability.

Risk-Free Rate (r): The interest rate of a risk-free investment, typically a government bond, over the option's life.

Dividends (q): For assets that pay dividends, this represents the dividend yield, which can affect the option's price.

Security Types with Options

Equity Options: Options on individual stocks or equity indices.

Futures Options: Options on futures contracts, allowing for the buying or selling of a futures contract at a set price.

Currency Options: Options on foreign exchange rates, allowing traders to hedge or speculate on currency movements.

Interest Rate Options: Options on interest rates, such as those for government bonds or interest rate swaps.

Commodity Options: Options on physical goods like gold, oil, or agricultural products.

Types of Options

Call Option: Gives the holder the right, but not the obligation, to buy the underlying asset at a specified price within a specified time period.

Put Option: Gives the holder the right, but not the obligation, to sell the underlying asset at a specified price within a specified time period.

American Option: Can be exercised at any time before expiration.

European Option: Can only be exercised at the expiration date.

Binary Option: Pays a fixed amount or nothing at all, based on whether a condition is met at expiration.

Exotic Option: Any option with a complex structure or payoff, such as Asian, barrier, or lookback options.

This list covers the fundamental concepts and terminologies in option trading, providing a solid foundation for understanding and navigating the options market.

Trader Type Definitions

Day Trader. A day trader engages in buying and selling financial instruments within the same trading day. Such traders capitalize on short-term market fluctuations, closing out all positions before the market closes to avoid unmanaged risk from overnight price changes. Day traders typically use leverage and short-term trading strategies to profit from small price movements in highly liquid stocks or currencies.

Swing Trader. Swing traders hold positions for several days to weeks to capture price movements or "swings" in the market. They typically look for opportunities where they can identify a clear price movement and then enter and exit their trades based on anticipated market trends. Unlike day traders, swing traders are less concerned with short-term market fluctuations and more focused on capturing larger movements over days or weeks.

Appendix C

Example Python Script to Find DITM Calls

Response with ChatGPT:

You can copy the script below into a file on your computer named find_ditm_calls.py and run it with Python:

python

CopyEdit

```
import yfinance as yf

import pandas as pd

import datetime

# List of stocks to analyze

stocks = ["AAPL", "MSFT", "NVDA", "TSLA", "AMD",
"GOOGL", "META", "AMZN"]

# Store results

results = []

# Date range

end = datetime.datetime.today()

start = end - datetime.timedelta(days=100)

for ticker in stocks:

try:

data = yf.download(ticker, start=start, end=end)

if data.empty:

continue

data['50_SMA'] = data['Close'].rolling(window=50).mean()

data['Change'] = data['Close'].pct_change()

data['RSI'] = 100 - (100 / (1 +
```

```
data['Change'].rolling(window=14).mean() /
abs(data['Change'].rolling(window=14).mean())))
current_price = data['Close'].iloc[-1]
sma_50 = data['50_SMA'].iloc[-1]
rsi = data['RSI'].iloc[-1]
pct_change_5d = (data['Close'].iloc[-1] - data['Close'].iloc[-6]) /
data['Close'].iloc[-6] * 100
# Filter based on technical criteria
if current_price > sma_50 and 40 < rsi < 70 and pct_change_5d
> 0:
results.append({
"Ticker": ticker,
"Price": round(current_price, 2),
"50 SMA": round(sma_50, 2),
"RSI": round(rsi, 2),
"5d % Change": round(pct_change_5d, 2)
})
except Exception as e:
print(f"Error processing {ticker}: {e}")
# Create DataFrame
df = pd.DataFrame(results)
print(df)
```